Building a Self-Evolving Organization

Building a Self-Evolving Organization

Leveraging Evolution to Prosper in an Environment of Constant Change

by

John A. Winder, PhD

Tru Publishing
Boise, USA

ISBN (paperback) 978-1-941420-35-5

22 21 20 19 18 1 2 3 4 5
1st edition, March 2018

Published by Tru Publishing - Boise, Idaho.

Cover & Interior Design: Tru Publishing
www.trupublishing.com

Editing: Robin Bethel, www.prosestudio.com
Editing: Kim Foster, www.kimfostereditor.com

For Patty—

Your love, kindness, and concern for others help fill the gaps in my character.

CONTENTS

INTRODUCTION

I live in a beautiful mountain community in the Idaho Rockies. From my deck, I have a wonderful view across a broad valley to the mountains beyond. And to borrow a line from Norman Maclean, "a river runs through it."[1] Along the river, there is an abundance of life. The fish in the river provide food for the bald eagles and osprey; waterfowl dine on river plants; bears, coyotes, foxes, and mountain lions forage and hunt along the river; and aspen, alders, ponderosa pine, and Douglas fir trees thrive.

But under the surface, things are not all that bucolic. This seemingly perfect environment is in a constant state of change. New plant and animal species enter this environment and compete with natives for resources; predators compete for prey and prey species must conversely protect themselves from predators; climate change is ushering in new diseases and parasites threatening both plants and animals; and a single wildfire can destroy, or at least alter, the environment for generations.

The first two decades of my career focused on studying living

---

1   Norman Maclean, *A River Runs through It* (Chicago: University of Chicago Press, 1976).

organisms as a researcher and university teacher, seeking to better understand how genetic change occurs in animals and plants. Later, I pivoted from studying organisms to leading, advising, and observing human-created organizations, including businesses; components of colleges and universities; state, federal, and local agencies; and not-for-profits. Though my early work as a scientist and professor may on the surface seem unconnected to my later work with these organizations, I found many parallels.

I discovered that many of the environmental pressures I witnessed in the natural world were also shared by the "operational environments" of organizations. The organizational habitat is undergoing constant transformation caused by dynamic markets; shifts in consumer and customer expectations; change in local, state, and federal policy; and availability of financial resources and other necessary inputs. At the same time, organizations are experiencing increased competition for customers and clients, inputs, labor, and financial resources. And there are increasing attacks by those seeking to steal intellectual properties (in other words, prey on the organization), syphon off the organization's resources (like a parasite), or directly damage or destroy the organization (as with disease). These pressures are ever present, constantly changing, and accelerating.

These similar pressures evoke comparable responses in both populations of living organizations and human-created organizations, allowing both to evolve when exposed to changes in their respective environments.

Scientists see evolution as a process by which living populations (interbreeding groups of individuals) change to meet the demands of a changing environment.[2] Some populations are more capable of making these changes, and they tend to prosper. Other populations

---

2   G. H. Hardy, "Mendelian Proportions in a Mixed Population," *Science* 28 (1908): 49–50; W. Weinberg, "Über den Nachweis der Vererbung beim Menschen," *Jahreshefte des Vereins Varterländische Naturkdunde in Württemberg* 64 (1908): 369–382; Charles Darwin, *On the Origin of Species by Means of Natural Selection* (New York, 1859).

may lack the ability to change, and they eventually go extinct. The differences between those populations that succeed under the pressures of change and those that fail are well understood and can be clearly documented.

To say that evolution is a powerful force is a gross understatement. In fact, human innovations pale in comparison to the achievements of evolution. It was evolution that created flight—enabling animals to not only fly, but to fly long distances, hover, and even fly backward. Evolution also led to fibers spun by spiders that are pound for pound much stronger than steel and venoms that can paralyze or kill prey. Many species, such as bats, some birds, dolphins, and whales, developed sonar-like systems as navigational aids. Of course, evolution's greatest accomplishment may have been the human brain—the thing that has allowed us to become self-aware and largely harness nature for our own purposes. There are literally millions and millions of examples of similar innovations in nature, and many are yet to be discovered.

Evolution allows populations to continually reinvent themselves to survive in an environment where change is the only constant. Populations of organisms that cannot reinvent themselves in response to environmental challenges (limited food sources, weather, competition from other species, disease, etc.) become extinct. Everything in nature is fluid. Nothing stands still. And living populations must continually evolve in order to survive. Much like natural populations of organisms, modern organizations must be nimble and capable of making appropriate changes in the face of their own environmental challenges. Failure to make these changes will lead to almost certain extinction. Understanding how natural populations evolve provides a blueprint that we can use to guide organizations facing the same unrelenting pace of change. Organizational extinction can be avoided by applying the same strategies used by every species on the planet.

Darwin thought that change was driven simply by natural selection,[3] but we have since learned that evolution is a bit more complex. There are actually six major evolutionary drivers, including the following:[4]

- Diversity—Differences in genetic makeup of organisms within the population.

- Mutation—The spontaneous creation of new genetic material caused by chemical change in the DNA molecule.

- Migration—The movement of genes into or out of a population as organisms migrate.

- Selection—The difference in contribution of genes to the next generation based on differences in "fitness" of potential parents.

- Isolation—The loss of diversity in small isolated populations caused by increased mating of relatives (inbreeding).

- Rate of Generation Turnover—The time required to replace one generation with the next.

In the coming pages, you will not only learn how these factors drive evolutionary change in nature, but you will also discover that the very same evolutionary principles can be directly applied to organizations of all types and sizes. And when you apply this knowledge in your organization, you will empower it to undergo rapid and thoughtful transformation in the face of change in your operational environment. This includes changes in your supply chain, budget allocations, customer preferences and service expectations, regulations, competition, and a whole host of other threats and challenges. In short, you will learn to enable your organization to "evolve" more rapidly and effectively and vastly increase the opportunity for a prosperous and impactful future.

---

3   Darwin, *On the Origin of Species*.

4   Hardy, "Mendelian Proportions," 49–50; Weinberg, "Über den Nachweis," 369–382.

"It is not the strongest of the species that survive, nor the most intelligent, but the one most responsive to change. "

Charles Darwin

CHAPTER 1

Change as the New Constant

If you are going to evolve your organization in response to changes in your operational environment, it is critical to understand the very nature of those challenges. Organizations face constant pressures caused by a number of factors ranging from small to large, temporary to permanent, local to global, organization-wide to civilization-shaking. Let's take a look at what some of this change may look like.

Internal and Cyclical Change Events

In our businesses, agencies, and not-for-profit organizations, we often focus on changes that are more internal or at least specific to our own operational environments. Many of these challenges are somewhat cyclical by nature and therefore can be anticipated, if not predicted. Budgetary shortfalls, new regulations and governmental policies, changes in customer preferences, the emergence of new competitors, upgrades to technology, and leadership transitions happen again and again. Dynamic organizations learn to plan for these events, respond as needed, and move on. Less nimble organizations will struggle through these challenges repeatedly and often become less and less viable with every downturn, eventually finding themselves on "the way to dusty death."[5]

Macro-Change Events

There are other change drivers that are more global in scope. Understanding these macro-change events is also critical to making your organization more resilient and more able to exploit future opportunities.

Macro-change events are often caused by broad-based innovation. Historians tend to categorize these innovations into major change "revolutions." While this phenomenon has existed from the very beginning of human history,[6] it's interesting to note there have only been a handful of these macro-change events over the past twelve thousand years—from the time that humans were widely dispersed hunter-gatherers until the present. Equally interesting is the fact that one of these major change events started in the mid-twentieth century and continues today.

I like to lump these macro-change events into three revolutions. The first was the advent of agriculture, often referred to as the "Agricultural Revolution," wherein farming and animal domestication made it possible to accumulate food surpluses. Consequently, fewer people were needed to produce food for the broader population. People who were not engaged in food production were then able to develop other specialized skills, leading to the creation of trades and interdependent communities. As the Agricultural Revolution unfolded over thousands of years—a slow disruption by today's standards—humans transitioned from hunter-gatherer societies to interdependent civilizations with viable governments, legal systems, and economies. This transformation paved the way for additional innovations, such as mathematics, science, and engineering.

Eventually, the application of mathematics, science, and engineering

5   William Shakespeare, *Macbeth* (New York: Dover, 1993).

6   Yuval Harari, Sapiens: *A Brief History of Humankind* (New York: Harper Collins, 2015).

became the catalyst for the second major driver of societal change—the "Industrial Revolution." This revolution gave rise to machines fueled by coal and petroleum products which supplanted animal power. Once more efficient and effective power was harnessed, factory-based production and long-range transportation of goods and people became reality. As a result, the world became increasingly interdependent, and change began to accelerate. Whereas the Agricultural Revolution occurred over thousands of years, the Industrial Revolution occurred largely within about two to three hundred years.

We are now in the third great revolution in human innovation, the "Digital Revolution" that began as humans developed effective telecommunications and computing technologies in the middle of the twentieth century. Since then, this revolution has changed virtually everything we do, from how and what we consume to how we do business, to how we work and recreate, to how we interact with one another. Digital technology has largely finished what the Industrial Revolution began—the establishment of a highly interactive global community. We now communicate, learn, conduct business, and exchange ideas as a global community.

Unlike the Agricultural Revolution which took place over thousands of years or the Industrial Revolution which took place over a few hundred years, the Digital Revolution has manifested massive amounts of change in a matter of decades. Additionally, the rate of change resulting from the Digital Revolution continues to accelerate.

The Accelerating Nature of Change in Digital Technologies

The "Digital Age" has been defined by our ability to build technologies that are better and faster and to do so at a remarkable rate of speed. This was predicted by Gordon Moore (cofounder of Intel), who in 1965 observed that the capacity of integrated circuits doubled every two years. This observation was labeled "Moore's Law." Moore expected the exponential rate of innovation to continue into the future, and this has so far proven to be accurate.[7]

Because of innovations in both hardware and software design, we have seen truly incredible increases in computing capacity since the mid-1960s. As a consequence, today's devices are literally millions of times more powerful than the devices available at the time that Moore put forward his hypothesis—and the trend shows no signs of abating.

Some have questioned, however, if our abilities to adapt to this rate of change (human adaptation) may be falling behind the level of innovation. In Thomas Friedman's book Thank You for Being Late, entrepreneur Eric (Astro) Teller expressed his belief that our ability to adapt to these technologies is advancing in a linear fashion that can't keep pace with the exponential rate of technological change predicted by Moore's Law. He further stated his belief that we have passed a threshold and we are now creating new technology faster than we can adapt these new tools. Teller suggested that without more effective education and governance, our ability to continue to leverage new technologies will be compromised.[8]

At the time of this writing, I am sixty-two years of age. During my professional career, I literally watched the Digital Revolution unfold. For much of that time, I (along with most of my colleagues) was always in want of the next "thing." It was not that we just wanted a new "shiny object," but that we always had applications we could not develop fully because of the technological limitations of existing computing platforms.

Yet I am now in general agreement with Astro Teller. Today, it seems that technology has moved beyond most of our immediate needs, and we are struggling to find uses for all of the new "stuff." To put

---

7   Gordon Moore, "Cramming More Components onto Integrated Circuits," *Electronics Magazine* 38, no. 9 (April 19, 1965).

8   Thomas L. Friedman, *Thank You for Being Late: An Optimist's Guide to Thriving in the Age of Accelerations* (New York: Farrar, Straus and Giroux, 2016).

this into perspective, we put the first men on the moon using computers that had less than one-millionth of the power of the iPhone 6s that is now in my pocket.[9] When both the processing power and the capabilities of software applications (apps) are considered, I am only able to use a very, very small fraction of my cell phone's capabilities. It seems that there is an app for everything today—the stuff we need, the stuff everyone else needs, and the stuff seemingly no one needs.

This deluge of innovation has already disrupted virtually all aspects of our lives and challenged what even a decade ago seemed like basic assumptions. Tom Goodwin, Senior Vice President of Strategy and Innovation at Havas Media provides a few stark examples from the business world, observing that "in 2015 Uber, the world's largest taxi company, owned no vehicles; Facebook, the world's most popular media company, created no content; Alibaba, the world's most valuable retailer, had no inventory; and Airbnb, the world's largest accommodation provider, owned no real estate."[10]

As technological change keeps accelerating, the Digital Revolution will continue to challenge our current ways of living and working—in ways we may currently find hard to imagine.

The Never-Ending Revolutions

While it may be tempting to focus on our current change revolution (the Digital Revolution), it is important to note that all three macro-change events (the Agricultural Revolution, Industrial Revolution, and Digital Revolution) continue. In fact, there appears to be no expiration date on any of these historic disruptions. The Agricultural

---

9   Tibi Puiu, "Your Smartphone Is Millions of Times More Powerful than All of NASA's Combined Computing in 1969," *ZME Science*, September 10, 2017, http://www.zmescience.com/research/technology/smartphone-power-compared-to-apollo-432/.

10 Tom Goodwin, "The Battle Is for the Customer Interface," *Tech Crunch*, March 3, 2015, https://techcrunch.com/2015/03/03/in-the-age-of-disintermediation-the-battle-is-all-for-the-customer-interface/.

Revolution lives on as we continue to innovate new methods of food production by enhancing and applying technologies developed in the Industrial and Digital Revolutions. Before the twentieth century, agriculture was the largest employment sector in the US, but by the 1960s, only 5 percent of the US workforce was engaged in agriculture (today it is less than 2 percent). As a result of increased mechanization and application of scientific farming methods and digital technology, agricultural productivity has continued to expand dramatically. Similarly, our abilities to innovate new industrial processes have been massively enhanced by the application of digital technologies, such as robotics, more effective inventory control, online marketing, and so forth.

All three major disruptions are intertwined and are still driving change. In fact, the rate of change in agriculture, industry, and technology is still accelerating. We are truly in an expanding universe whereby innovation drives change and change drives additional innovation and so on and so on.

Ramifications of Macro-Change Events

We owe a lot of our current quality of life to these major revolutions, but each has yielded its own negative outcomes. The Agricultural Revolution laid the framework for civilization, but larger and more compact communities created environments ideal for the transmission of disease. Early cities experienced multiple outbreaks of bacterial and viral diseases that ravaged their populations. These were not significant problems among hunter-gatherer societies that were more dispersed and were therefore less likely to transmit disease across the larger population.

The Industrial Revolution resulted in environmental pollution as coal and other fossil fuels began to be used as major energy sources. Use of fossil fuels from the beginning of the Industrial Revolution to the present has also led to elevated atmospheric carbon dioxide levels causing climate change and may yet result in the greatest environmental crisis in human history. Waste products from manufacturing plants have also polluted waterways. Even though major efforts have been made to clean up rivers and streams, many still contain residues of industrial pollutants. Furthermore, the growth of massive industrial complexes led to exploitation of labor which also created fertile ground for the two world wars and the rise of communism in the twentieth century.

Though the negative effects of the Digital Revolution are only starting to be recognized, we can surmise that there will be many ramifications ahead. We have already seen revolutions in the Middle East facilitated by social media, a new criminal element focused on stealing digital data, jobs being replaced by robots, blowback from those displaced by globalization, disruption of the press and broadcast media by online information sources, and a dumbing down of political discourse to fit into short sound bites and social media posts.

Rapid change makes many people long for the way things used to be. Much of the 2016 presidential election seemed to focus on a return to the good old days when labor-intensive industries, such as coal extraction, steel production, and manufacturing, were the norm. However, the technology genie is out of the bottle. Modern plants employ fewer individuals possessing more advanced skills. Automation has made modern factories safer, more efficient, and more globally competitive. Product quality has also been vastly improved by the application of robotics and other forms of automation.

My crystal ball is pretty fuzzy today. I often struggle to understand the ramifications of emerging technologies, like autonomous vehicles and the impact of having everything interconnected through the internet. But history suggests we should heed Astro Teller's recommendations. We need to strive to keep pace with technological advancement, and we need to get busy developing public policy and educational systems that prepare our workforce for the jobs of the future instead of looking backward. This should extend into every workplace. To be successful, managers must make an unprecedented effort to prepare workers to leverage coming technologies.

Managing under Constant Change

Because of the rapid rate of change in their operating environments, many organizations are questioning long-standing norms, such as leadership models, communication processes, employee development, and evaluation and reward systems. In his book The Future of Work: Attract New Talent, Build Better Leaders, and Create a Competitive Organization, Jacob Morgan described five types of organizational structures. Most of these have arisen as organizations attempt to address and harness increasing rates of change in their operating environments:

1. **Traditional Hierarchies**—Military-type structures where workers are managed as cogs in a machine, with decisions being made by a small group of elites with little or no feedback channels from workers to management. Strict hierarchies still exist in many small organizations and in family-run businesses. These also persist in the military, but even the US Army is questioning rigid structures in an era of rapid and constant information flow.[11]

2. **Flatter Organizations**—Largely hierarchical organizations but with channels opened to allow workers to interact and exchange ideas, and, to some degree, provide feedback to management. Management maintains strong oversight but is more informed by feedback from employees, customers, and other stakeholders. Examples of organizations with this structure include Cisco, Whirlpool, and Pandora.

3. **Flat Organizations**—Often referred to as "self-managed" organizations where each person is considered to be equal and no job titles exist. Employees can work on any existing

---

11 Wilson A. Shoffner, The Military Decision-Making Process: Time for Change (monograph for School of Advanced Military Studies, US Army Command and General Staff College, Fort Leavenworth, KS, First Term AY 99-00), file:///C:/Users/Owner/Downloads/ADA381816.pdf.

project they choose or even initiate their own projects, but they are responsible for securing funding and building their own team. While this system has merits, it tends to lead to a degree of chaos and lack of accountability in many cases. Success has been observed in small organizations, but scaling to larger structures has been difficult. Valve, a gaming company, is cited as an example of how this system can be successfully implemented.

4. **Flatarchies**—Structures that fall between traditional hierarchies and flat organizations. These are often hierarchies that allow formation of ad-hoc teams where team members are free to function as equals, exchange ideas, and innovate. However, they may also retain elements of flat organizations whereby structured teams are formed by management to address specific tasks. This system has been widely implemented by large innovative corporations such as 3M, Google, Adobe, and LinkedIn.

5. **Holacratic Organizations**—Organizations that allow for distributed decision-making and permit individuals to do what they do best. Structure is provided in what is referred to as "circles" or departments. Information is openly distributed through organizational meetings. Zappos and Medium are companies that have employed this structure.[12]

It may be an understatement to say that organizational structures are struggling to keep up in a high-change environment, but there seems to be an overriding desire to eliminate barriers to communication, expand collaboration, and drive innovation.

The struggle to optimize interaction between management and employees also extends to organizational planning processes. In many organizations, planning processes are still conducted entirely within the executive suite. This top-down planning is time efficient,

---

12   Jacob Morgan, *The Future of Work: Attract New Talent, Build Better Leaders, and Create a Competitive Organization* (Hoboken, NJ: John Wiley and Sons, 2014).

but often overlooks the innovative ideas of employees. Therefore, top-down plans tend to be short on imagination. Morale can also be compromised when employees—especially the most creative employees—feel that they do not have a stake in determining the organization's future.

Since the 1960s, organizations have sought alternatives to top-down planning. Dominant among these was a concept that came to be labeled as "strategic planning." Eventually, this approach was practiced in all sorts of organizations (businesses, public agencies, and not-for-profits).[13] The greatest attraction of strategic planning was that it allowed for broader input, including internal and external analyses, capturing opinions from stakeholders, reaching consensus on a vision for the future, and developing steps necessary to achieve this vision. But in high-change environments, strategic planning has proven to be too slow and therefore often results in plans that are functionally obsolete on day one.[14] Also, because of the importance of consensus building in the strategic planning processes, the final product tends to emphasize the status quo over progressive transformation.

Organizations are seeking new paradigms in their leadership structures and planning methodologies that enable them to respond to change more rapidly and effectively; but most of these efforts are still falling short. And this is why it's time to now turn to the well-established processes for dealing with change by emulating nature. These natural processes have been tested by fire in constantly changing environments for billions of years.[15]

---

13   Phillip Blackerby, "History of Strategic Planning," Blackerby Associates, accessed November 9, 2017, http://www.blackerbyassoc.com/history.html.

14   Shoffner, *Military Decision-Making Process.*

15   Gary L. Neilson, Bruce A. Pasternack, and Decio Mendes, "The Four Bases of Organizational DNA," *Strategy + Business* 33 (Winter 2003), http://www.strategy-business.com/article/03406?gko=4f38.

"It is not necessary to change. Survival is not mandatory."

W. Edwards Deming

CHAPTER 2

Analogs between Nature and Organizations

Over my career, I have been fascinated to observe how organizations behave much like living entities. They consume resources and strive to grow and multiply. Some evolve into something much different. And some—many, in fact—contract, decline in influence, and even go extinct. Once I began to ask myself what was different between those that were successful and those that were headed toward contraction or extinction, I began to recognize that the fundamental difference was the quality of the ideas that were expressed in the organization. As I looked more closely, I came to understand that ideas in organizations behave very similarly to genes in natural populations.

Ideas as the Genes of Organizations

In nature, genes can be created spontaneously through mutation; they can be favored or eliminated by natural selection; they can move into or out of a population when individuals who possess them migrate; they can interact with other genes in multiple ways to control complex biochemical processes, such as growth, reproduction, and immune response; and they can be lost when populations become small and isolated. These elements are the major drivers of evolution in natural populations.

Similarly, ideas can be generated spontaneously; they can be selected for expression or eliminated by management; they can enter or leave organizations; and they can interact with other ideas in multiple ways to address complex problems or opportunities. Furthermore, ideas, like genes, can be lost when organizational subunits become small and isolated. This results in more uniform thought processes as idea diversity is lost. Ultimately organizations that lose diversity become less able to evolve in the face of change in their operational environments.

Vessels and Reservoirs of Genes and Ideas

I further recognized that many other elements of organizations had similar analogs in nature. Employees are analogous to the members of natural populations (organisms). Employees are the source of all intellectual property possessed by an organization. They are essentially vessels full of ideas. In nature, individual organisms are essentially vessels of genes.

Now let's widen the lens a bit more. From a geneticist's perspective, a population is a group of intermating individuals—a "reservoir" of genes. We can similarly think of an organization as a reservoir of interacting ideas.

In nature, the sum of all similar natural populations composes a species. Generally, members of the different populations that make up a species are physically able to intermate but may be kept from doing so by distance or other geographic barriers. From time to time, these boundaries are overcome and individuals from one population may enter another population.

Organizational categories—or, in other words, organizations with similar missions and outputs—are very similar to species. For example, there may be multiple grocery stores in your community. They operate separately but tend to have a similar function: selling food and related items. Individuals working in one grocery store have the skills that allow them to move to a store owned by another company, taking with them their ideas and experiences. Yet, as in nature, there are often barriers to these movements, such as distance, company policy, retirement plans, and so on.

Ecosystems

You may recall from your high school biology class that ecosystems are composed of interacting organisms and nonliving elements, such as minerals, atmosphere, and sunlight, which are needed to sustain life. Natural ecosystems can occupy small or large geographic areas, with boundaries that tend to ebb and flow. Individual species can also occupy multiple ecosystems.

Many organizational theorists like to use the term "organizational ecosystem" to describe the overall environment that an organization operates within. An organizational ecosystem is similar to natural ecosystems in that it is essentially an interacting group of organizations, including suppliers, competitors, regulators, customers, and threats. The physical "space" occupied by an organizational ecosystem also lacks rigidity and tends to expand and contract as new opportunities and restrictions that affect organizations within the ecosystem arise.[16]

When opportunities are favorable, organizations may expand into other communities, states, or countries. Some of us may remember when most grocery stores were locally owned and operated within a single community. The size of their ecosystem was quite small— maybe no larger than the boundaries of their neighborhood or community. Today, most grocery stores are part of regional, national, and even international conglomerates. They also sell much more than food, offering a multitude of goods and services under one roof. The size of the ecosystem occupied by grocery stores has expanded dramatically. When new competition arises, new restrictive regulations are imposed, or economies contract, organizations may

---

16   James F. Moore, *The Death of Competition: Leadership and Strategy in the Age of Business Ecosystems* (New York: Harper Collins, 1996).

move out of geographic areas. In this case, their organizational ecosystem may get much smaller.

To help you visualize these analogies, I have summarized the major analogous elements of natural systems and organizations in the following table.

Natural Populations	Human Organizations
Gene—The fundamental unit of inheritance	Idea—The fundamental unit of innovation
Organism—An individual member of a population (a reservoir of genes)	Employee—An individual member of an organization (a reservoir of ideas)
Population—A group of inter-breeding organisms	Organization—An individual business, public agency, or not-for-profit
Species—The sum of all populations of similar organisms capable of intermating and producing fertile offspring	Organizational Category—The sum of all organizations with similar missions and outputs
Ecosystem—A community of interacting organisms and elements of their physical environment: • Producers—Organisms that convert light, oxygen, and carbon dioxide into sugars and provide nutrients to other organisms in the ecosystem • Consumers—Organisms that consume other organisms, such as herbivores, predators, and scavengers	Organizational Ecosystem—A network of interdependent organizations: • Suppliers—Groups or individuals that provide raw resources and capital to the organization • Customers—Consumers of products produced by the organization • Competitors—Organizations that compete for the same resources and customers

Natural Populations	Human Organizations
Ecosystem—A community of interacting organisms and elements of their physical environment (continued): • Competitors—Organisms that compete for the same resource base • Decomposers—Organisms that break down waste and dead organisms • Parasites and disease agents • Abiotic Components—Nonliving elements, such as water, air, minerals, and atmospheric temperature	Organizational Ecosystem—A network of interdependent organizations (continued): • Waste Disposal—Entities that remove and decompose waste from organizations • Threats—Entities that seek to advance their status by damaging other organizations • Regulators—Organizations providing oversight over other organizations in an effort to prevent damage to the ecosystem

By defining parallels between natural systems and organizations, we have set a stage. We can now delve deeper into how nature responds to environmental change and how you can make your organization more responsive in the face of new opportunities and challenges. We will begin by examining the very composition of your organization and the importance of the diversity of the ideas generated by your employees.

"One good analogy is worth three hours discussion."

Dudley Field Malone

CHAPTER 3

Why Diversity Is Critical to Nature and Organizations

Have you ever wondered why some organizations seem to readily modernize and restructure in the face of change? Conversely, have you watched other organizations hunker down and steadfastly resist change—essentially backing into the future with both eyes clearly focused on past glory, while largely ignoring future challenges and opportunities? In short, some organizations have abundant energy to move to the next level, while others simply lack the "fuel" for change.

This fuel for change is diversity—diversity of genetic makeup in nature and diversity of ideas in organizations.

Genetic Diversity: The Fuel for Evolution

In nature, observed differences among individuals can be due to either variation in their genetic makeup (nature) or due to variations in the environmental circumstances of their lives (nurture). Since variation among individuals caused by the environmental circumstances is not inherited, it has essentially no impact on the evolutionary processes. But conversely, difference in the genetic makeup of individuals allows populations to change and is truly the fuel for evolution.

When genetic variation is lacking, there is minimal difference between the most adapted and the least adapted individuals. Genetically uniform populations are therefore unable to evolve rapidly enough to avoid extinction in the face of environmental change.

One great example of how genetic diversity protects species from extinction was observed in the peppered moth. At the beginning of the Industrial Revolution, virtually all of the peppered moths in the British Isles exhibited a mottled grayish color. This allowed them to blend into the colors of native trees and elude predators. Then the Industrial Revolution arrived, and burning of wood and coal increased. This created a layer of soot on tree trunks and just about everything else. The grayish-colored moths became very easy for predatory birds to see and capture. Fortunately, there were either a few black peppered moths around, or perhaps a mutational event occurred creating a new dominant gene for black color. Nevertheless, moths carrying at least one copy of this gene were black. These individuals blended into the new surroundings, evaded predators, and thrived in the new environment. Before long the vast majority of peppered moths were black.

Then the environment changed again. Pollution was mitigated and air quality improved. Vegetation returned to its original native color. The black moths became easily visible to predators. Fortunately for the species, there was still genetic variation in this trait because the mottled-grayish gene was recessive and masked when paired with the dominant black gene. This provided an opportunity for the peppered moth to evolve back to its original mottled grayish color and again blend into its surroundings.[17] Therefore, genetic variation in the color gene saved this species not once but twice.

Idea Diversity: The Fuel for Change in Organizations

Just as natural populations without adequate genetic diversity are

17   H. B. D. Kettlewell, "Further Selection Experiments on Industrial Melanism in the Lepidoptera," *Heredity* 10 (1956): 287–301; Kettlewell, "Darwin's Missing Evidence," *Scientific American* 200 (1959): 48–53.

destined to fail, organizations without a diversity of ideas will also falter. This is especially true under conditions of constant and rapid change in the operational environment.

Since employees are the vessels holding ideas, we can expand the diversity of ideas by broadening the diversity of the workforce through effective recruitment and retention practices. We often hear about diversity in the context of race, ethnicity, gender, and sexual preference. But if our goal is to increase the diversity of ideas within an organization, we should consider additional sources of difference among the workforce as well. This includes diversity of experience, personality type, geographic origin, education, skills, personal interests, and even political viewpoints. The diversity of ideas possessed by employees can also be expanded by providing more diverse opportunities for learning and professional development. I will touch more on this later.

A diverse workforce is more likely to bring forward fresh new ideas to address challenges and opportunities. Thus, diversity increases the likelihood that the best solution is in the mix. The value of diversity is rapidly becoming apparent when we look at the founders and senior executives of some of America's largest corporations. According to Robert Lenzner, fully 40 percent of the largest US companies were founded by either immigrants or their children. This includes stalwart companies, such as Proctor & Gamble, Pfizer, and U.S. Steel, and also more recently established tech giants, such as eBay, Google, and Brightstar.

Additionally, Lenzer pointed out that 25 percent of high-tech companies established between 1995 and 2005 had at least one immigrant founder. He further pointed out that three-fourths of all companies receiving US venture capital have at least one foreign-born senior team member, such as the CEO, CTO, or VP.[18] A McKinsey and Company study noted that as ethnic diversity of

---

18   Robert Lenzner, "40% of the Largest US Companies Founded by Immigrants or Their Children," *Forbes Magazine*, April 25, 2013.

senior executives rises, there is an associated rise in earnings before interest and taxes (EBIT). This amounted to a 0.8 percent increase in profits for each 10 percent increase in diversity.[19]

But the value of diversity extends far beyond the executive suite. In healthy organizations, ideas are generated and advanced by employees from across the organization. Diversity among these individuals is critical. McKinsey and Company contrasted the financial performance of companies in the top quartile for diversity to those in the bottom quartile. Companies with the highest rates of gender diversity outperformed those with the lowest rate of gender diversity by 15 percent. More significantly, companies in the top quartile for ethnic diversity outperformed those in the lowest quartile for ethnic diversity by 35 percent.

Diversity and inclusion are not just HR functions. Often the overall culture of the organization must change in order to create a positive environment that encourages a diverse workforce. If this is lacking, employees with diverse backgrounds will not feel comfortable and will move on.

The principles of inclusion should radiate throughout all aspects of the organization. Everyone should be well aware of the values derived from diversification of the workforce and the leadership team. Organizations should set specific goals and measurable benchmarks related to diversification of the workforce and celebrate reaching those benchmarks. They should also consider making diversity a major component of their brand identity and generally not be satisfied until their workforce and leadership team mirror the diversity of those they serve.

As essential as it is to have a diversity of ideas, it is not in itself the entire solution; the organization must also have mechanisms in place that allow for ideas to be shared and advanced. Communication

---

19   Vivian Hunt, Dennis Layton, and Sara Prince, "Why Diversity Matters," McKinsey and Company, January 2015, http://www.mckinsey.com/business-functions/organization/our-insights/why-diversity-matters.

structures are critical as is the overall administrative structure of the organization. Earlier, I discussed management in an era of constant change and how organizations are exploring new models to improve idea sharing and teamwork. But employing a new organizational model is no panacea. In order to honor and exploit the value of diversity, you must ensure that ideas flow freely. Top-down hierarchical organizations often lack mechanisms for ideas to bubble up to decision makers, and barriers can also be created within departments and locations anytime that the flow of ideas is restricted. I will pursue this issue in more detail in the next chapter.

"Diversity is the engine of invention. It generates creativity that enriches the world."

Justin Trudeau

Steps You Can Take to Increase Workforce Diversity

1. **Recognize that diversity extends beyond race, gender, and ethnicity.** The following list provides major categories to consider, but there may be other diversity components worthy of consideration within your organization.

   - Gender and gender identity
   - Race
   - Ethnicity
   - Sexual preference
   - Experience
   - Personality type
   - Geographic origin
   - Source of education
   - Skills
   - Personal interests
   - Religion
   - Political viewpoints
   - Physical ability

2. **Do not limit your recruitment to a few colleges and universities just because they have provided satisfactory employees in the past.** You may be missing some new ideas and approaches.

3. **Expand the geographic scope of your recruitment efforts.** You will reach more candidates and tap into new ideas and viewpoints.

4. **Recognize that creating and maintaining a diverse workforce are a constant process.** It is not only about hiring but also about supporting diverse workers. Set goals and measure your progress toward achieving these goals. Constantly evaluate the success of your diversity initiatives.

5. **Recognize that diversity is not simply about slogans; it is about action and creating a culture that supports a broad base of ideas and experiences.** Consider the workplace culture honestly and discretely gather feedback from employees, asking the following questions:

   • Does your organization promote inclusiveness?

   • Are there attitudes or actions in your organization that create divisions?

   • Are divisions adequately addressed?

6. **Monitor retention rates among employees representing all diversity categories.** Seek to understand why individuals leave the organization and take appropriate action to mitigate any problems.

7. **Strive to create a diverse management team.** This brings new ideas into the decision-making process and clearly demonstrates that the organization is focusing on inclusion and creating opportunities for advancement for all.

8. **Strive to create flexible work schedules.** This creates opportunities for the organization to tap into talent that may not be able to work in a more rigid workday. Also consider if jobs could be effectively conducted via telecommuting. This allows individuals to contribute to the organization while also taking care of children and other family needs.

CHAPTER 4

How to Overcome Isolation

E ven when there is an abundance of idea diversity, elements of separation and isolation can still exist. This may be due to the physical distance between branches of an organization, a perceived necessity to protect trade secrets, the organizational culture, the administrative structure, or even the design of workplace facilities.

Isolation seldom leads to positive outcomes. In this chapter, I will examine the ramifications of isolation in nature and in organizations and what can be done to overcome these "pitfalls."

The Pitfalls of Isolation

One of the greatest hazards to the survival of living organisms occurs when they exist in small and isolated populations. Under these conditions, relatives are more likely to mate. As a consequence, members of isolated populations become increasingly more related (inbred) and genetic diversity is lost. Inbreeding also leads to a loss of vigor, called inbreeding depression. Since small isolated populations lack diversity and are less vigorous, they are unable to evolve rapidly in the face of environmental change.

About thirty years ago, I visited the Bishop Museum in Honolulu.

At the time, there was a major exhibition in place that provided an overview of the impact of settlement on the flora and fauna of the Hawaiian Islands. As a geneticist, I was immediately drawn to the interpretive displays.

The exhibition described the amazing number of species that had been driven to extinction or to the brink of extension. The reasons for this were twofold. First, island populations were isolated from others by the vast Pacific Ocean, and because of inbreeding, they lacked diversity. Second, human settlement resulted in a rapid change in the environment. Settlers introduced new species that preyed upon or competed with existing species, and since the predators and competitors had evolved in larger continental populations, they were generally more fit (competitive).

In isolated natural populations, the number of breeding individuals may shrink and then expand again as environmental quality declines and subsequently improves. Geneticists label the shrinking of the size of the breeding population as a "bottleneck." When a population is in a bottleneck situation, very few individuals may be contributing genes to the coming generations. In some species, a single male (or a small group of males) may be siring virtually all of the offspring for several years. These individuals are often labeled "founders" because of the disproportionate genetic influence they have on future generations.

Isolated organizations are subject to many of the same challenges. In an article in the *Harvard Business Review*, Scott Anthony described a process that he called "innovation inbreeding." He outlined how innovation in small isolated organizations tends to be largely uninspired and is often led by the same individuals over and over, which tends to lead to a narrow and fairly uniform idea "bank" within the organization. The smaller and more isolated the organization, the greater the likelihood of flawed innovation. Anthony also observed that breakthrough ideas do not occur in isolation. Alternatively, fertile ground for innovation is created when individuals with different backgrounds and skills interact.[20]

I have experienced the effects of isolation in different types of organizations throughout much of my career. The impacts of segregation tended to be most prevalent in small organizations and with larger organizations segregated into many small isolated subunits. This included small businesses, public agencies, and not-for-profits. I was amazed how many characteristics they shared. Here is my short list.

1. **Isolated organizations generally lack the ability to innovate.** Often ideas that are generated in isolation fail because they contain flaws that go unrecognized due to a lack of critical review. These spontaneously generated ideas are much like mutated genes. They simply lack the merit to replace existing concepts.

2. **Behavior and thought processes tend to be very uniform and often reflect a dominant personality within the organization.** These dominant individuals create what is analogous to the "founder effect," whereby their influence is greatly exaggerated relative to others. The ideas of these individuals are more likely to be supported by the organization and to "suck up all of the oxygen in the room."

3. **The organization as a whole tends to be unable to respond effectively to changes in their operational environment.** This eventually leads to failure, though some of these organizations hang on for a long time. This is especially the case for public organizations and not-for-profits.

4. **There is often a culture that supports the notion of some sort of "magic sauce" within the organization.** Isolated organizations may lack the ability to critically appraise themselves. Instead, they often develop a sense of superiority over competitors. This attitude is largely unfounded.

---

20 Scott Anthony, "Stop Inbreeding Innovation," *Harvard Business Review*, March 30, 2012.

5. **Failure to change is justified based upon the perception of past successes.** Managers and employees stress that they have always done things a certain way and see no need to change.

6. **New employees often come to the organization from nearby.** Often individuals begin as interns or part-time employees and then later move into full-time employment. There is a lot of emphasis placed on new hires fitting into the organizational culture and "getting along." New employees are often mentored by long-term employees from the "founder" class and therefore indoctrinated to the idea norms of the organization.

Ending Isolation and Reinvigorating the Organization

In small isolated natural populations, the lack of diversity limits the opportunity for evolutionary change. As long as the population remains isolated, the only means by which diversity can be increased is through gene mutation. But gene mutation occurs at a very low rate, and the outcomes are very unpredictable. Additionally, most mutations are not beneficial, and some are outright harmful.

Let me offer an analogy. I have a spot in my garage where I keep tools and hardware that I need (or think I need) to maintain our home. I try to keep like things organized in containers and bins. Each category (screws, bolts, plumbing stuff, etc.) is stored together. But it seems that I am constantly and randomly accumulating stuff over time that just doesn't fit into any of my categories. I usually don't throw these items away, so I have to find a place to store them. They end up in a general bucket that I keep for any as yet unidentified future needs. They are not immediately useful, but I keep them just in case.

Mutations are like my bucket of miscellaneous items. Mutated genes are generally not immediately useful because they occur randomly, and in order to be valuable, they would have to replace an existing gene that has evolved over thousands of years of evolution. All populations have these buckets of mutated genes that are stored in the genomes of their component organisms. Evolution draws upon these "buckets" to allow species to change over time. But because genes mutate at a fairly low rate, the size of the bucket of miscellaneous genes depends on the size of the population. In small populations, the bucket is smaller and offers few solutions. In larger populations, the bucket is bigger and possesses more options for change.

Other evolutionary forces also fail to act effectively in small isolated populations. As long as the population is isolated, migration is nonexistent. Additionally, natural selection doesn't work very well because the individuals within an isolated population are so similar that one does not have an advantage over any other. The bottom line is that small isolated populations do not evolve very effectively. When the environment changes rapidly and dramatically, these populations are doomed.

But there is one viable approach to remedy the detrimental effect of isolation. You may have already realized this. We simply need to find the means to break down the barriers that created the isolation in the first place. To dramatize this, let me use a real-world example based upon my own experiences as a youth. I believe this will clearly demonstrate both how isolation is created in living populations and how this isolation can be readily overcome.

I grew up on a cattle ranch in southwestern New Mexico. Ranches in this region are very isolated, and ranch headquarters are often five to ten miles apart. Ranchers tend to keep a small number of barn cats (less than twenty) to control mice in livestock feed storage areas. Because of the distance and the presence of predators in the space between ranches, few if any cats successfully migrate from one ranch to another. Therefore, cats exist at each ranch as small isolated populations. Often one dominant tomcat will sire all of the offspring for several consecutive years.

Over time, inbreeding increases within these isolated cat populations. As expected, they then become less resistant to parasites, diseases, and any predators that sneak onto the premises. They also begin to look more "ratty" and unthrifty. Their reproductive rates decline, and as a result, the population becomes further reduced. The cats become much less effective at catching mice and rats. In short, they exhibit all of the classical symptoms of inbreeding depression.

When ranchers begin to see this level of decline in the cats, they realize that action is needed if they want to save their cat population. Fortunately, the solution is very easy and effective. All they need to do is bring in a new dominant tomcat from another population. The introduction of the new tomcat gives rise to an effect called hybrid vigor, which is simply recovery from the depressive effects of inbreeding among the next generation of cats. Consequently, the next generation will be more vigorous and more effective "mousers." It only takes a very small amount of migration (one tomcat every few years) to completely arrest the impacts of inbreeding and genetic isolation.

Some ranchers actively pursue tomcats from outside sources with proven abilities to catch mice. In doing so, they go beyond simply arresting inbreeding and are also importing new genes for mouse-catching ability with these new tomcats. They may also choose to increase the number of new cats added to the population to increase diversity. After all, there is more than one way to skin a cat . . . or should I say to catch a mouse? A diverse population of barn cats will likely bring more approaches to the table and be even more effective at catching the vermin.

The depressive effects of idea inbreeding can be fatal to the organization in much the same way that inbreeding depression can destroy living populations. Organizations can leverage migration to offset the impacts of "idea inbreeding" in a similar way. Just as the ranchers were able to arrest inbreeding by importing new genes into their cat population, managers can arrest idea inbreeding by importing new ideas into their organization. The bottom line is that idea inbreeding is the result of isolation and the inability to bring new ideas into an organization and/or effectively share ideas once they enter. When new ideas are allowed to enter an organization and to move effectively throughout the organization, innovation is the logical outgrowth. Modern organizations must be dynamic. This can only happen when a large and expanding pool of viable ideas are present.

Like the ranchers who pursue tomcats with proven abilities, plant and animal breeders heavily leverage migration in order to improve crop and livestock species. They have long recognized that it is important to introduce the very best genetic material into their breeding populations. Therefore, they often "expand their population" by seeking the best of the best—literally traveling the world in pursuit of potential immigrants to add to their population. Breeders also seek new genes from other species or even across kingdoms (transferring genes from plant to animals and vice versa)[21] by leveraging cutting-edge molecular biology techniques.

Ideas migrate in much like genes and similarly overwhelm the negative effects of isolation. Individuals entering an organization (as new employees, guest speakers, external trainers, etc.) can bring with them ideas that have been developed elsewhere. Additionally, existing employees can expose themselves to the ideas of others by reading, attending meetings, and engaging in online discussions and other forms of interaction and, through this process, bring ideas into the organization. Some organizations also force idea migration by rotating individuals among different locations and units as a standard method of operation.[22]

Of course, migration can also go the other direction whereby ideas leave an organization. This most often occurs when creative employees seek greater challenges, opportunities, pay, or recognition by moving to another organization. Out-migration of ideas can also occur when existing employees share their ideas with others through publication,

---

21 "Genetically Modified Animals," Reuters, July 25, 2013, http://www.reuters. com/news/picture/genetically-modified-animals?articleId=USRTXTZ7A.

22 Jeanee Nienaber Clarke and Daniel McCool, *Staking Out the Terrain: Power Differentials among Natural Resource Management Agencies* (Albany, NY: State University of New York Press, 1985).

presentations, collaborations, and other forms of professional exchange. Some organizations embrace the sharing of ideas outside of the organization while others seek to keep this intellectual property a closely held secret.

The very same tools that have allowed plant and animal breeders to leverage migration to massively change domesticated species can be used to improve the number and quality of ideas held by an organization. When employees seek ideas that are substantially different from those held by the base organization, the organization maximizes the difference between existing ideas and migrating ideas. Similarly, when a greater proportion of employees seek new ideas from outside sources, the organization expands the proportion of migrating ideas relative to native ideas.

The difference between the ideas migrating into the organization and the native ideas of the organization can be maximized when employees extend themselves and pursue new concepts. Earlier, I mentioned how animal and plant breeders "expand the population" by reaching further and further in pursuit of new genetic material. The same concept exists in organizations.

In my mind, one of the greatest challenges to Western democracy is the desire to seek out other like-minded individuals. We are seeing the emergence of a new form of tribalism whereby individuals increasingly receive information from comfortable sources that reinforce their beliefs. In doing so, people tend to ignore or discount other views, approaches, and potential solutions. If employees continually pursue ideas from the same sources, the likelihood of new concepts entering the organization is diminished. Conversely, if employees are encouraged to pursue ideas outside their comfort zones by attending meetings outside of their area of expertise, reading materials that foster new lines of thought, and simply engaging with individuals who have different life experiences, then new ideas will flow into the organization.

Earlier, I discussed the importance of diversity in driving change in organizations and in natural populations. Too often management hires individuals who fit into the organization's culture or comfort zone. I have frequently heard managers discuss how they preferred to hire graduates from specific universities because they integrate readily into the organization. While technical competency is important in new hires, this can be achieved while also diversifying the workforce. When new employees come from a variety of colleges and universities, their ideas, skills, and knowledge are also migrated into the organization, expanding the organization's diversity. In today's environment, this diversification is critical to an organization's ability to change and prosper in a dynamic environment.

Create Churn

In many organizations, efforts have been underway to increase diversity. But being a diverse organization is only part of the solution. You must also find ways to encourage the interaction of ideas across the organization. When barriers between units and individuals are breeched, creativity is stimulated and exciting collaborative ventures can happen.

In a sense, the creation of a collaborative concept in an organization is like making bread. Before you can create "effective" bread, you have to go to the store and buy a variety of diverse ingredients. These are then "migrated" into your pantry. But just because you now have all of the ingredients doesn't mean that you have the final product. You have to put the diverse items (flour, yeast, water, salt, and other ingredients) together in the proper proportions, mix appropriately, and then bake for the right amount of time.

Complex ideas often require multiple migrations of ideas. Though the ingredients were purchased at the grocery store, their origins were more varied and distant (whether from a wheat farm, salt mine, etc.). Ideas will enter an organization through different channels and will be carried by different people.

These often disparate ideas then need to come together in the right blend to yield the raw product. Some of these ideas will play a larger role than others, but all will be important to the final product. After all, flour is the largest ingredient in bread, but it is not bread without small critical components, such as salt, yeast, and other ingredients.

It is absolutely vital that mechanisms be in place to facilitate the mixing or churning of these ideas. This allows multiple people to add elements, critique, and refine. In some organizations, all of this churning will take place internally. This can take many different forms, such as designed multidisciplinary teams, forums and seminars, and even informal gatherings. Many organizations even design "churn" into their buildings and facilities by creating common spaces where people can informally meet and exchange ideas.[23]

Then comes the baking. Some concepts are not ready once all of the ingredients are assembled. They may need to bake and cool until the timing is right, until adequate resources are available, or until the market is ready in order to be fully viable.

When people work across disciplines, locations, and even organizations, the weaknesses in an individual idea are more likely to be exposed and overcome. Additionally, when ideas from diverse sources come together in the right proportions, the outcome is almost always greater than the sum of its parts.

We often credit individuals with great creations as if they worked alone, but this has seldom been the case. For example, Leonardo da Vinci was once thought to have unilaterally created many innovations during the late fifteenth and early sixteenth centuries, including the parachute, flying machines, armored vehicles, repeating canons, and a self-propelled cart, among many other things. However, recent evidence suggests that many of these ideas were not original at all.

---

23   Amy Moore, "Complete Guide to Apple Park," Macworld, September 25, 2017, http://www.macworld.co.uk/feature/apple/52-facts-about-apples-spaceship-campus-february-drone-video-3489704/.

Instead, they were refinements of ideas developed by others earlier.[24]

When you consider any successful human innovation, you will find that it was not created in a vacuum. Inventors such as Savery (credited with the steam engine), the Wright Brothers (flight), and Edison (electric lights) were all informed by the ideas of others. I would even hazard a bet that the invention of the wheel was most likely a collective effort.

"We don't function well as human beings when we're in isolation."

Robert Zemeckis

---

24 "Leonardo, the Man Who Saved Science," *Secrets of the Dead*, PBS, aired April 5, 2017, http://www.pbs.org/wnet/secrets/leonardo-man-saved-science-preview/3462/.

Steps You Can Take to Overcome Isolation and Foster Greater Collaboration

1. **Create a more diverse workforce.** As mentioned in chapter 3, diverse organizations tend to be more creative and successful than more uniform organizations. Creation of a diverse workforce requires a concerted and continuous effort on the part of the organization as a whole. When diversity is expanded, the idea pool is also expanded. Conversely, if you hire like-minded people, you constrain innovation.

2. **Flatten your organizational structure and encourage teamwork.** Rigid hierarchies tend to lead to structures that limit interaction among individuals residing in separate departments or units. Alternate structures include flatter organizations, flat organizations, flatarchies, and holacratic organizations. (Revisit chapter 2 for more details.)

3. **Increase internal interaction.** In larger organizations, "tribes" tend to form when the structure is segregated into subunits that do not effectively interact. Managers can form diverse multidisciplinary teams to develop new concepts, product designs, and so forth. These teams should have representation from all relevant components of your organization (finance, engineering, sales and marketing, production, design, maintenance, IT, etc.) This allows ideas to flow more effectively within the organization. However, these teams should not be considered to be permanent structures. Teams can become insular over time and risk creating new isolated tribal structures wherein idea inbreeding occurs within the teams.

   Managers can also seek opportunities for more casual interactions. One concept that is largely rooted in the Silicon Valley is the development of office space that forces individuals to interact on a constant basis. This can be facilitated by creating common areas, causeways, and dining facilities that entice individuals to interact and collaborate with others with different backgrounds and ideas.

Finally, technology can be leveraged to ensure that ideas are shared among employees. Recurring webinars, conference calls, and other technology-mediated approaches can be valuable tools for helping individuals throughout the organization learn about the ideas of others.

4. **Increase external interaction.** Many organizations deliver training and other forms of professional development internally. In these cases, exchanges are limited to ideas that are already present in the organization. Alternatively, when employees are allowed to seek ideas outside of the organization, the opportunity for new ideas to enter the organization is greatly increased. But even when organizations encourage external engagement, employees may be tempted to attend meetings and training programs that are well within their comfort zones. Employees (including managers) should be encouraged to stretch themselves and seek opportunities for engagement outside of their disciplinary focus. Great products come from bringing disparate ideas together. While CEO of Apple, Steve Jobs recognized this as he married software and hardware with design principles to create the iPhone and other platforms.[25] Many of these concepts had their origins outside of the company. We too must recognize that most great ideas reside outside of our organizations and not within.

5. **Bring external experts into your organization.** Ideas can be very efficiently imported when consultants, guest speakers, and other visionaries are engaged to work with your employees. This is often the most time- and cost-effective way to import ideas because you can expose a large number of people to new concepts within a short period of time. This limits travel

---

25   Walter Isaacson, *Steve Jobs* (New York: Simon and Schuster, 2011).

time and expense and lost productivity. The downside to this strategy is that it is not very "organic." Someone must decide the topics and the purveyors of ideas to invite. Biases can be created when these decisions are based on the opinions of a few persons within your organization.

6. **Move key employees to new posts within the organization.** In organizations with isolated subunits, this has helped to churn the idea pool and to avoid idea inbreeding. For example, the US Forest Service is largely divided up into small administrative units called districts, which are generally led by professional managers called rangers. Early on, the agency was concerned about the tendency of isolated rangers to develop ideas in isolation and even deviate from organizational areas of focus. To avoid this, a process was developed whereby rangers are expected to migrate from district to district throughout their careers. This not only limits the potential for idea stagnation in individual districts but also facilitates movement of ideas throughout the broader organization.[26]

7. **Increase involvement of external stakeholders in visioning and planning processes.** Often customers are the first to recognize problems and opportunities for product improvement. Similarly, other stakeholders, such as suppliers, lenders, and retailers, can provide new ideas and dynamic feedback that can lead to overall process improvement.

---

26   Nienaber Clarke and McCool, *Staking Out the Terrain.*

CHAPTER 5

Selection: How Genes and Ideas Get Advanced

When ideas emerge within an organization, some will be immediately ready for application, some will be less mature and need more tweaking, while others will have major issues and need to be discarded altogether. Management, at some level, is charged with making this decision. This can be a daunting task, and the careers of leaders often hinge on their abilities to recognize and support great ideas while avoiding those with critical flaws.

One of the best analogies for idea selection can be seen when plant and animal breeders seek to improve the genetic merit of domestic plants and animals. The process they use is called artificial selection. This is accomplished by deciding which individuals will be allowed to become parents of the next generation. Let's examine how this process works, including the many challenges and pitfalls that breeders encounter along the way. Then let's use this knowledge to enhance your ability to find and advance truly great ideas within your organization.

How Genes Get Selected by Nature

Natural selection is largely the mechanism by which the environment exerts its influence on the genetic makeup of a population or species. As the environment changes, pressures on living organisms also change. Some cope better than others and leave more progeny. The ability of an individual to pass its genes to the next generation is called "fitness."

A very fit individual possesses genes that are preferred under specific environmental conditions. It really doesn't matter whether an individual is prettier, bigger, or faster. What matters is whether the individual can produce more offspring that then become parents of subsequent generations. It is the challenges created by the environment that ultimately determine which individuals are most fit. Fitness is not a constant; individuals who excel under one set of environmental constraints may lose their superiority when conditions change.

How Plant and Animal Breeders Determine Fitness

As I mentioned previously, plant and animal breeders exercise artificial selection by controlling which individuals become parents. In other words, breeders supplant the environment and directly determine which individuals are most fit. When done properly, this can be a powerful tool leading to genetic improvement.

However, breeders often make mistakes, and their decisions then lead to unintended consequences. This occurs when genes associated with a desired characteristic also code for other undesirable traits. For example, domestic turkey varieties in the US have been selected for more breast meat, and as a result they have such large muscles that they can no longer mate naturally. In these varieties, all mating is done by artificial insemination. These unintended consequences have been observed in virtually all species that have been exposed to selection pressure by plant and animal breeders. Over time, breeders tend to recognize these pitfalls and become more informed and sophisticated in their approach. But a lot of damage can be done along the way.

In domestic populations under aggressive selection pressure, genetic variation may be eventually exhausted. This is especially the case when breeding objectives remain constant over time. In essence, all of the good genes (relative to the breeding objectives) get concentrated in the population, and all of the less desirable genes relative to the breeding objectives are removed by selection. This creates more uniform populations. But when environmental conditions (or selection goals) change, these populations may simply lack the genetic variation necessary to change. This has become a major issue in many domestic species. In some cases, so much genetic diversity has been lost due to artificial selection that food production systems have been compromised. This concern is so grave that the US Department of Agriculture maintains seed and tissue banks. These banks are reservoirs of genes that would otherwise have been lost under the pressures of artificial selection. When environmental changes occur, breeders can tap into these banks to reintroduce genetic diversity into domestic crop and animal varieties.[27]

How Ideas Get Selected

Much like plant and animal breeders, managers of organizations determine the fitness of ideas. I like to break this down into three critical functions related to both the creation and advancement of ideas. First, management is responsible for setting a stage whereby creativity can flourish. This includes hiring a diverse and creative workforce, supporting professional development, establishing effective teams, and properly rewarding creativity in performance reviews. The second key function of management is deciding which ideas are allowed to be expressed and become part of the organization's product/service mix and which ideas will be set aside. The third role played by management is to support and advocate for those ideas that have been selected.

---

27   To learn more about the steps that are being taken to preserve the genetic diversity of both plants and animals, visit https://www.ars.usda.gov/plains-area/fort-collins-co/center-for-agricultural-resources-research/plant-and-animal-genetic-resources-preservation/.

In organizations, idea selection is often used to reduce variation and to create focus. However, overly rigid idea selection can also exhaust idea variation to the point of bringing change to a halt, a phenomenon often seen when decisions are highly centralized and controlled by a select few individuals. In today's dynamic environments, this sort of centralization limits an organization's ability to respond to change and makes failure much more likely.

As is the case in plant and animal breeding, errors often occur when management selects ideas. Accidents frequently happen, and unintended consequences result. These accidents arise when those making decisions do not adequately assess potential risks associated with an idea and when decision makers allow their own biases to taint the decision-making process. History is chock-full of examples of idea selection leading to unintended consequences in business, governments, not-for-profits, and even in personal lives. Here are a couple of examples from the business world.

In the early 1980s, IBM was the dominant manufacturer of mainframe computers. But small desktop personal computers were beginning to emerge, most of which were produced by small companies. As no one company had yet emerged as the dominant player,[28] IBM saw an opportunity and decided to rush a new line of computers to the market.[29] This was accomplished within a year. The new machines (IBM PCs) were very well received, and the product release became a pivotal event in the personal computer revolution. Because IBM was focused on quickly developing and releasing the product, two critical ideas were advanced that would later be shown to have unintended consequences for the company.

First, IBM decided to enter into an agreement with an upstart software company to provide operating system software for its new

---

28   "The Television Program Broadcast Transcripts: Part II," *Triumph of the Nerds*, interview by Robert X. Cringely, PBS, aired June 1996, http://pbs. org/nerds/part2.html.

29   "The Birth of the IBM PC," IBM, accessed November 9, 2017, https:// www- 03.ibm.com/ibm/history/exhibits/pc25/pc25_birth.html.

platform. The agreement also allowed this upstart to develop and sell additional software to operate on the new platform. Second, IBM chose to use an existing firm to produce the microchips for their new computer. By making these two decisions, IBM decided not to take a significant equity stake in the two things that provided the "brains" of the new computers (software and microchips), which left IBM with a hardware platform that was easily copied by other companies. Oracle's Larry Ellison called IBM's decisions "the single worst mistake in the history of enterprise on earth."[30]

Fast forward to today, and we can see the ramifications of the selection of these ideas. The software company that provided the operating system and subsequent software for the IBM platform was Microsoft. Today, Microsoft's market capitalization is over one-half trillion dollars. The chip manufacturer selected by IBM was Intel. Today, Intel's market capitalization is about $170 billion. Today, IBM no longer manufactures personal computers and has a smaller market capitalization than either Microsoft or Intel ($162 billion).

In the 1970s, the Eastman Kodak Company (Kodak) developed a prototype digital camera. The company recognized the potential for the device and decided to invest billions into additional research and development.[31] However, there were key individuals within the company who were very nervous about the impact of this technology on their traditional film and photo paper sectors, so the decision was made to essentially table the digital technology in favor of their traditional product lines. By the time Kodak recognized they had selected the wrong idea, the digital photography industry was off and running. They never caught up, and in 2012 Kodak filed for bankruptcy.

There are numerous other examples of the unintended consequences of idea selection, examples which extend far beyond the business

---

30   PBS, "Television Program Broadcast Transcripts."

31   Sam Gustin, "In Kodak Bankruptcy, Another Casualty of the Digital Revolution," *Time Magazine*, January 20, 2012.

world. Leaders of nations, not-for-profits, and public agencies also routinely employ or reject new ideas only to later realize that they were in error. While no one is infallible, there are some who seem to be more effective in determining what ideas within their organization will be expressed.

I have worked with many managers, and there has been tremendous variation in how they approached the task of determining which ideas would be advanced and which would be set aside. Some prided themselves in being very decisive and making decisions quickly. Unfortunately, a number of decisive individuals were also quite reckless in making idea selections without having a complete understanding of benefits and risks. Confidence is a powerful attribute when it is paired with good analytical skills; however, managers who are confident but prone to shooting from the hip can be very dangerous to an organization's success. One of my former colleagues framed this group when he said that they are "often wrong but never in doubt."

At the other end of the spectrum, there are the managers who seek to eliminate all risk by continuously analyzing an idea. In the meantime, an opportunity slips away. These individuals are plagued by another malady—paralysis by analysis.

Obviously, the best manager is one who can come to a timely decision about an idea and at the same time fully understand the risks and rewards. I have come to recognize that these good managers possess a unique form of "brain power."

Generally, brain power can be placed into six categories. Each has its own relevance to an organization.

- Knowledge—The theoretical or practical understanding of facts, information, and skills resulting from education and experience
- Skill—The ability to perform tasks well
- Intelligence—The ability to acquire knowledge and skills

- Creativity—The ability to create and recognize new ideas, forms, methods, or interpretations
- Problem-Solving Ability—The ability to find solutions to difficult or complex problems
- Wisdom—The ability to take actions or make decisions by exercising pertinent experience, knowledge, and good judgment

I have worked with leaders and managers who were brilliant people. Some were highly skilled in certain aspects of their jobs, while others were exceptionally creative and able to effectively solve many problems. However, when it came time to select ideas, the most effective managers were wise above all else. Wisdom entails elements of several forms of brain power. You must be able to tap into knowledge and experience, but you also must be capable of exercising good judgment. You have to be able to determine when someone is feeding you a line and when someone is expressing an authentic and valuable idea.

There is a certain level of humility associated with wisdom; wise leaders recognize what they don't know. This leads them to seek additional information and advice. Additionally, a wise person has a good feel for when to act quickly and when to wait for the proper time to execute an idea.

Wise managers have multiple feedback loops that they leverage to better understand risks and reward potential. This includes getting feedback from customers/clients, employees, and other stakeholders. Too often I have seen feedback loops established to endorse the manager's decision instead of informing the decision. Advisory structures must be composed of individuals with appropriate insights and experiences and not of individuals who are simply advocates of management.

Obviously, no manager can be expected to analyze and decide on every idea emerging in her or his organization. Senior managers must learn to see themselves more as the person on the rudder and less as an organizational filter. A rudder enables the craft (the organization) to maintain a course toward its destination. Whereas a filter exhibits absolute control over which elements are allowed to pass and which are removed, the person on the rudder does not exert control over all functions of the vessel. As was the case with IBM and Kodak, when the wrong filter is deployed, too many good ideas may be discarded and too many bad ideas may get through. Modern management needs to create a much more organic environment where new well-informed ideas flourish and help the organization evolve.

"Leadership is the art of giving people a platform for spreading ideas that work."

Seth Godin

Steps You Can Take to Ensure that the Right Ideas Are Selected and Advanced

1. **Strive to be the leader on the rudder instead of a filterer of ideas.**

   - Focus on moving the organization toward long-term goals and toward achieving specific objectives.

   - Avoid becoming an absolute filter that rigidly determines which ideas are given life and which are killed. Give latitude to employees and allow them to collectively develop and test ideas.

   - Create an environment where innovation emerges from a collaborative environment, where ideas arise and are subsequently debated, modified, and combined with complementary concepts.

   - Seek to broaden and diversify those engaged in the decision-making process.

2. **Set the stage for creativity to flourish.**

   - Hire and support a diverse workforce (see chapter 3).

   - Support learning and professional development across the organization.

   - Establish effective teams.

   - Effectively reward and recognize creativity.

3. **Evaluate ideas in an unbiased and analytical manner.**

4. **Once ideas have been selected, monitor their implementation and help those responsible to overcome organizational hurdles.**

   - Too often new ideas are approved by a small number of senior managers. Often these managers' biases may lead to the rejection of meritorious ideas. Leverage other individuals in the process of approving new ideas.

5. Make decisions in a timely manner.

- Avoid paralysis by analysis, but also take care to understand the ramification of each idea. There is a balance that must be struck between speed and due diligence.

6. Never underestimate the importance of wisdom within the management team.

- Wise leaders not only possess knowledge and experience but also have the ability to exercise good judgment and to recognize what is factual and what is false or misleading.

CHAPTER 6

How Dominance and the Environment Cloak the Merit of Genes and Ideas

In a perfect world, the merit of genes and ideas would be apparent and easily recognized. However, this is rarely the case. The value of both genes and ideas can often be distorted or even totally hidden. Let's now examine how this occurs and what steps can be taken to gain a clearer view of the true merit of the ideas emerging in your organization.

Dominance: How One Gene Affects Another

In higher organisms, genes generally occur in pairs (called alleles), and these paired genes are not always equally expressed. Sometimes paired genes are identical, and sometimes they are different. When paired genes differ, one gene can exert "dominance" over its allele (pair). Dominance describes the degree that paired genes interact. Sometimes both are expressed fully, and sometimes only one allele is expressed. The degree of this interaction, also called the degree of dominance, can vary from none to a very strong interplay between the genes. Let's consider some examples of varying degrees of dominance and how this affects natural and artificial selection processes.

First, let's look at an example whereby both alleles are expressed. In this case, a plant breeder can identify the genetic makeup of the individual based upon its outward appearance.

The color of snapdragon flowers is controlled by a single pair of genes.[32] Flowers can be red, pink, or white depending upon the type of genes that are present. When two genes for the red color are paired, the flower is red; when two genes for the white color are paired, the flower is white; when a plant has one red gene and one white gene, the color falls between red and white and is pink. In this case, both genes are expressed and you can distinguish the genetic makeup of each plant by its appearance. If you consider pink to be exactly halfway between red and white, **no dominance** is present and both genes are equally expressed. But if pink snapdragons have slightly more red pigment than white pigmentation, some degree of dominance would be present. This condition is called **partial dominance.**

Often one gene completely masks the effect of its allele. This is called **complete dominance.** When this occurs, the masked gene has no effect on the outward appearance or function of the organism. Here are two examples of traits in humans that express complete dominance:

There is a genetic lung disease in humans called cystic fibrosis (CF.) Only individuals with two copies of the CF gene contract the disease. Historically, most of these individuals die by late adolescence and therefore do not reach reproductive age, which means there is almost absolute natural selection pressure against these individuals. But those with only one copy of the CF gene are healthy and indistinguishable from those who possess two normal genes; therefore, natural selection does not act upon the individual who is a carrier of one CF gene and one normal gene. Even though the CF disease is largely fatal, the CF gene has avoided elimination by natural

---

32 "Some Phenotypes and Their Explanations," Indiana University, accessed November 9, 2017, http://www.indiana.edu/~oso/lessons/Genetics/Phenotypes.html.

selection by hiding behind its dominant allele (the normal gene). After all, the average fitness of individuals who carry no CF genes and those who carry only one copy of the CF gene is equal. Complete dominance fools natural or artificial selection and allows less desirable or even dangerous genes to be retained in a population.[33]

Another interesting example of complete dominance is the Paisa gene that causes early-onset Alzheimer's disease in some communities in South America.[34] The disease is generally fatal and expressed in individuals in their mid-40s. In this case, the mutant gene is dominant to the normal gene, so all individuals with either one or two copies of the gene will exhibit Alzheimer's disease. But interestingly, even though Alzheimer's disease is fatal, natural selection has not been able to eliminate this defective gene. The reason for this is that it is not expressed until after most individuals reproduce, and therefore carriers pass on the gene before they exhibit symptoms.

There is one additional mechanism by which paired genes interact. This is called **overdominance**. This occurs when individuals possess one copy of the more dominant gene and one copy of the more recessive gene.

There is a condition in humans called sickle cell disease (SCD.) Individuals carrying two copies of the SCD gene experience a form of anemia caused by misshapen red blood cells, which have a propensity to clump and not flow effectively through blood vessels. Individuals with one copy of the SCD gene are normal. At this point, this looks a lot like complete dominance with the normal gene totally masking the SCD gene. But there is another wrinkle— individuals who carry the SCD gene are also resistant to malaria.

In tropical environments, individuals carrying one copy of the normal gene and one copy of the SCD gene have an advantage: they do not

---

33 "About Cystic Fibrosis," Cystic Fibrosis Foundation, accessed November 9, 2017, https://www.cff.org/What-is-CF/About-Cystic-Fibrosis/.

34 "PSEN1 E280A (Paisa)," Alzforum, accessed November 9, 2016, http://www.alzforum.org/mutation/psen1-e280a-paisa.

exhibit anemia AND they are resistant to malaria. They are more fit than those possessing two normal genes or two SCD genes. These individuals are called heterozygotes. Natural selection favors these heterozygotes over those with either two normal genes or two SCD genes (homozygotes). Therefore, natural selection tends to favor both the normal gene and the SCD gene simultaneously.[35]

It is important to remember that in most cases both natural and artificial selection act upon the outward appearance of an individual. An individual organism's fitness is a reflection of not only the genes they possess but also how those genes interact. Additionally, environmental effects, such as previous nutrition or disease exposure, may increase or diminish an individual's fitness. Selection is not always "smart" enough to determine if an organism's fitness is due to the total value of its genes, how those genes are paired, or its past environment.

Managing Idea Dominance

As is the case in natural populations, idea selection acts on the outward appearance of ideas. In a perfect world, managers would select only the ideas with the greatest fitness—those that increase the organization's viability to the greatest extent. But the true value of a concept can be masked by other ideas and tempered by managers' experiences and biases. Often, preference is given to those concepts that are well presented and have easily recognized value. But bias can be introduced when the originator of an idea creates a "dominance effect" in order to overshadow competing ideas. This is often the case when the originator or his/her advocates are effective marketers and political operatives.

Sometimes dominance is complete and an alternative idea may be totally masked (complete dominance), and sometimes the dominance may be partial with alternative ideas being noticed but not fully

---

35   Thomas N. Williams and Stephen K. Obaro, "Sickle Cell Disease and Malaria Morbidity: A Tale of Two Tails," *Trends in Parasitology* 27, no. 7 (2011): 315.

expressed (incomplete dominance). It is even possible that two or more ideas may be fully expressed (no dominance). Of course the optimal situation is when multiple ideas come together and yield an effect that is greater than the sum of their parts (overdominance).

In most organizations, product lines and service strategies are composites of many ideas. Often, a few great ideas (component parts) can carry the day and determine whether a new product line or service is moved forward. These great ideas, however, may hide some other flawed ideas that are not immediately apparent. That was the case with the IBM example. The company had some really great ideas; the IBM PC platform was truly revolutionary. But the company leadership was so preoccupied with building and delivering a product that was head and shoulders above the competition that they failed to realize other defective ideas were being carried forward. They decided to not exercise control over the intellectual property associated with chip design and software application. In doing so, they gave away something that proved to be many times more valuable than their entire corporation. Managers must recognize the existence of dominance when making decisions as to which ideas are advanced within the organization.

I once worked with a passionate individual (let's call him Jim—not his real name). Jim had a knack of getting his ideas advanced within the organization. He had a strong personality and knew how to engage management to successfully sell his ideas. Unfortunately, those ideas frequently failed to deliver on their promise over time and ultimately resulted in the expenditure of significant resources to solve problems created by Jim's concepts. Though there were individuals who presented alternative concepts at the time, these were totally masked by the dominance of Jim's ideas and never saw daylight.

In a sense, Jim's ideas tended to possess characteristics similar to the Paisa gene that causes early-onset Alzheimer's disease in humans. Remember that selection has little impact on this gene because it is not expressed until after individuals produce offspring. Similarly, the flaws in Jim's ideas were often not seen for years after implementation. Because of the long timeline between initiation and failure, sometimes Jim was not even connected to the debacle. And worse yet, his ideas often spawned offspring with similar problems before the initial flaws were exposed.

Managers need to recognize that dominant ideas may not be the best ideas. Effort needs to be made to hear from those who lack the political and marketing skills to advance alternative ideas. Perhaps someone at IBM had the idea that the company should build its own software and chips for its personal computer line. If this did occur, it was set aside in favor of the path that IBM management chose (to outsource these enterprises to Microsoft and Intel). In essence, the idea was not fully expressed in the company. If that idea could have been fully expressed, who knows, IBM may have become the largest and most profitable company on the planet.

Perhaps the most compelling outcome is seen when two or more ideas come together to yield an effect that far exceeds the independent value of each idea. This is similar to our earlier example of overdominance in SCD. Recall that individuals possessing two copies of the SCD gene experience a severe form of anemia. Individuals with two normal genes do not have the disease, but they are susceptible to malaria. Those with one copy of the sickle cell mutant and one normal gene have a huge advantage of being resistant to malaria without displaying anemia. Let's take a look at an example of **overdominance** from the business world.

Dr. Spencer Silver was a researcher developing adhesives for 3M. He came upon a compound called "microspheres," which had a "removability characteristic" that allowed one object to stick to another surface without leaving adhesive residue on the surface after it was removed. Silver realized he had a novel concept but struggled to marry it to an idea that would be commercially viable. The adhesive was just too weak for most traditional applications.

Meanwhile, another 3M scientist named Art Fry had become frustrated during his weekly church choir practices. He would bookmark songs in his hymnal with small pieces of paper. But if he was not careful, the bookmarks would fall out of the hymnal, and he would lose his place. If he used typical adhesives, such as tape, it would damage his book. As a scientist, he began to brainstorm mechanisms to address the problem. He then recalled a seminar that he had attended at 3M on Silver's adhesive. Suddenly, the light went on. If he could apply Silver's adhesive to small pieces of paper, his problem would be solved. Fry then collaborated with Silver to develop the Post-it Note.[36]

In this case, two ideas came together in a very synergistic manner. In nature, this would be considered overdominance, whereby the combination of two ideas produced an outcome that far exceeded the sum of the two ideas taken separately. Silver's idea—his discovery of microspheres—did not seem to have an application. Fry's idea—a bookmark that stayed in place—needed the right mechanism. When combined, these two ideas yielded one of the most profitable lines in 3M's history. The value of each idea by itself was negligible, but the combination of the two ideas produced something that was greater than the sum of its parts.

Effective managers learn to recognize how ideas interact. This includes understanding when one idea masks or dominates others and when two or more ideas may come together in a complementary manner. They need to be able to isolate the quality of an individual idea from the background noise created by dominance exerted by others with competing ideas. Finally, they must be able to isolate the value of the idea from environmental noise. Environmental noise occurs when competing ideas are presented by individuals with access to differing levels of resources.

---

36   "History Timeline: Post-it Notes," 3M, accessed November 9, 2017, http://www.post-it.com/3M/en_US/post-it/contact-us/about-us/.

Why Genes and Ideas Work in One Environment but Fail in Another

One of the greatest errors made by plant and animal breeders is to assume that individuals with superior genetics in one environment will also excel elsewhere. This phenomenon is called "genotype by environment interaction." Over time, breeders have learned that varieties must be developed under the conditions in which they will be utilized.

As you travel from south to north, animals of the same species tend to change dramatically. In more southern regions, they will be much smaller than those in northern habitats. In warmer climates, animals that can dissipate heat have an advantage. In colder climates, those that can retain heat have an advantage. Larger animals are more capable of retaining heat while smaller animals are more efficient in dissipating heat. Over time, natural selection has optimized the genetic composition for each specific environment. Therefore, the genes possessed by the black bear which evolved in New Mexico would not necessarily be conducive to survival in British Columbia.

Frequently, ideas are often not transferable from one organizational environment to another. While some ideas may have largely universal value, others may work extremely well under one set of circumstances only to fail elsewhere.

Liberal democracy is one of those great ideas that works extremely well under some environments but fails horribly in others. This is an idea that seems to require some specific conditions to truly thrive, such as a highly effective constitution, highly informed voters, universal suffrage, respect for the rights of others, minimal corruption, and rule of law, among others. From its beachhead in the United States, there have been many attempts to expand democracy to other countries. When the environment is conducive, democratic governments have been very successful, but when the key prerequisites for democracy are absent, the track record is not so pretty. We have all likely seen ideas that were not transferable from one organization to another. Sometimes we understand why and sometimes we don't.

Often timing can be everything. If the environment isn't right for the expression of the idea, then it just doesn't work. For example, Leonardo Da Vinci is largely credited with the invention of the parachute. This was a truly novel concept, but it had essentially no application at the time. Those living in the 1500s would have likely considered the idea useless. It wasn't until human flight was perfected before the value of the idea was recognized.[37]

Sometimes an idea that has been successful in a smaller organization is applied unsuccessfully in a larger, more complex organization. We often hear politicians promise to make government agencies work like a business; yet to date, this approach has largely failed. I attribute this to the fact that many of the critical drivers in the private sector are simply absent in public agencies.

Understanding environmental difference is key to understanding whether an idea can be successfully migrated into an organization. Careful analysis is necessary to understand how the organization differs from the environment where the idea originated.

Sometimes there will be naysayers who use any minute difference between organizations as an excuse for rejecting a new idea. Differences will exist, but that doesn't necessarily mean that the idea cannot be applied. But generally, an idea will need to be tweaked to some degree to successfully fit into a different organization.

The ability to understand how both dominance and environmental differences cloak the expression and effectiveness of ideas is key to accurately deciding which will be advanced, which will be tabled, and which will be discarded. The following chapter will focus on this process in more detail and provide specific guidelines that will help you become a better decision maker.

---

37   PBS, "Leonardo."

*"The culture of the dominant class hinders
the affirmation of men as beings of decision."*

Paulo Freire

Steps You Can Take to Overcome Cloaking and to Identify the Best Ideas

1. **Do not allow dominant personalities to dominate others.** Just because someone is the loudest or even the most persuasive, do not assume that their ideas are necessarily superior.

   - Strive to give voice to the introverts, remembering that some of the most creative people are reserved and reluctant to blow their own horn.

   - Create venues that allow these individuals to express their thoughts and ideas.

2. **Recognize when innovators are being suppressed by their peers.**

   - Understand that change challenges the status quo. Some employees will apply pressure on others with creative ideas to keep them in line and to keep things in a more constant state.

3. **Recognize that ideas that work in one environment may not necessarily be successful elsewhere.**

   - Your organization's ecosystem may be much different. The skills and knowledge of employees, available financial resources, customer/client demands, competitors, regulations, and external threats may create constraints or opportunities that were not present in other organizations.

   - Also recognize that ideas that work elsewhere may have merit in your organization. Examine carefully and consider how tweaking these ideas can make them useful within your environment.

CHAPTER 7

Supporting the Best Ideas to Benefit the Organization

The task of identifying the best ideas shares a lot of characteristics with work that I did earlier in my career. At the time, my efforts centered on finding ways to accurately compare the genetic merit of animals reared in vastly different environments. Environmental variation caused by such things as differences in food quantity and quality, weather, and exposure to diseases creates a lot of noise that masks an animal's true genetic potential, which makes it difficult to compare individuals reared in one place to those reared in another. Additionally, dominance is a major factor that can cause some genes to be partially or fully masked by more dominant genes. We used complex mathematical algorithms to analyze data on tens of thousands of animals to account for these biases and allow us to make direct comparisons among animals reared in thousands of locations across the US. Interestingly, a very similar approach is now used by the NCAA to create rankings of college football teams playing in numerous different conferences across the country.

I bring this up because a manager's or leader's task can often seem equally daunting. They are often charged with determining how limited resources will be used to the maximum benefit for the organization. In short, they must decide which ideas will be supported and which will be tabled or discarded—and they do not have a magic algorithm to help them separate the wheat from the chaff. In order to accomplish this, they need to acquire as much data as possible and seek to access the strengths and weaknesses of each concept. They also need to exercise their own judgment. Frequently, the careers of leaders rise or fall based on their ability to bet on the right idea. To increase the probability of choosing successful ideas, potential for error must be mitigated without engaging in perpetual analysis.

I find that rubrics can be very useful in helping managers reach the best decision when considering new ideas and concepts. This process requires individuals who present new ideas to management to participate in an exercise that requires critical thought and analysis. This also shifts much of the analytical responsibility for analysis from management to those proposing the idea.

Insight Assessment provides good general guidelines for developing a similar rubric for use in educational settings.[38] This process leans heavily upon earlier work, such as the Delphi Report.[39] I find these approaches are very informative. We can build upon these ideas to create a structure that can aid in the evaluation of ideas in the workplace.

In essence, a rubric forces users to use critical thinking principles to advance their idea. Whether used formally or informally, this structure can be extremely important in assessing the value of ideas and in

---

38   "The Holistic Critical Thinking Scoring Rubric—HCTSR," Insight Assessment, accessed November 9, 2017, HCTSR+2014+Insight+Assessment%20(5).pdf.

39   Peter A. Francione, *The Delphi Report—Critical Thinking: A Statement of Expert Consensus for Purposes of Educational Assessment and Instruction*, Insight Assessment, November 1989, https://www.researchgate.net/profile/Peter_Facione/publication/242279575_Critical_Thinking_A_Statement_of_Expert_Consensus_for_Purposes_of_Educational_Assessment_and_Instruction/links/5849b94508ae82313e7108de/Critical-Thinking-A-Statement-of-Expert-Consensus-for-Purposes-of-Educational-Assessment-and-Instruction.pdf.

limiting the potential for errors.[40]

The following is my rubric which focuses on evaluating the merits of a specific idea. The user may be a manager. But in many cases, I would suggest that those proposing ideas be asked to use the rubric when developing their proposals. This would expand the use of critical thinking in the development and presentation of new concepts, products, processes, and so forth.

Do those originating and presenting the idea (proponents) possess appropriate knowledge and experience?

Very Weak	Unacceptable	Acceptable	Strong
Little evidence existed that proponents had the knowledge or experience necessary to develop a viable idea.	Significant gaps existed in relevant knowledge and/or experience of proponents to develop a viable idea.	Proponents possessed adequate experience and knowledge necessary to develop a viable idea.	Proponents possessed in-depth experience and knowledge related to the idea.

Was supporting evidence for the idea presented?

Very Weak	Unaccepetable	Acceptable	Strong
Evidence was consistently biased or blatantly inaccurate.	Evidence was often misinterpreted.	Evidence was generally relevant and accurately presented.	Evidence was consistently accurate and highly relevant.

Was supporting evidence obtained in a similar environment?

Very Weak	Unaccepetable	Acceptable	Strong
Evidence came from circumstances that were not applicable to the organization.	Evidence came from circumstances that were largely not applicable to the organization.	Evidence came from circumstances with significant overlap with the organization.	Evidence came from circumstances that largely mirrored the organization.

---

40 Thomas Gilovich, *How We Know What Isn't So* (New York: Simon and Schuster, 1991).

Were both pro and con arguments for the idea identified?

Very Weak	Unaccepetable	Acceptable	Strong
Relevant counter-arguments were not identified or were hastily dismissed.	Strong and relevant pro and con arguments were often lacking.	Most of the relevant pro and con arguments were identified.	Pro and con arguments were consistently identified.

Were the idea and alternatives effectively analyzed?

Very Weak	Unaccepetable	Acceptable	Strong
Alternative ideas were consistently ignored or superficially evaluated.	Alternative ideas were often ignored or superficially evaluated.	Most alternative ideas were accurately analyzed and evaluated.	All alternative ideas were thoroughly analyzed and evaluated.

Were conclusions about the idea correct and supported by appropriate data?

Very Weak	Unaccepetable	Acceptable	Strong
Conclusions were uniformly based on incorrect, biased, irrelevant, and unwarranted claims.	Conclusions were mostly based on incorrect, biased, irrelevant, and unwarranted claims.	Conclusions were warranted and based on appropriate data and analytical methods.	Conclusions were judicious and based on appropriate data and analytical methods.

The goal with this rubric is to help identify the strengths, shortcomings, and critical flaws in a proposed idea. Since an idea can be proposed by anyone within an organization, the rubric needs to be very adaptable and work for scientists and engineers, as well as line workers and office staff. With minor customization, if needed, this general structure should be useful for a wide range of organizations.

Stagnation: When New Ideas Are Summarily Killed

Often when organisms migrate into a new population, some may carry genes that are less desirable in the new environment. Natural selection acts upon these genes, and over time most will be eliminated. The rate at which they are removed depends upon the degree to which the genes affect fitness. Sometimes, the rate at which these genes enter the population will roughly equal the rate that they are removed by selection, which results in equilibrium between the effects of migration and selection. Under this condition, the effects of gene migration are entirely offset by the effects of selection. Therefore, the migration of these new genes into the population has no net effect.

Obviously, leadership cannot support every new idea that migrates into an organization. Some will be flawed, and some may fall outside the mission of the organization. It is a legitimate role of management to set aside these ideas (select against them). However, it is also possible for leadership to completely stifle new ideas if virtually every new idea entering the organization is eliminated by negative selection pressure. An organization in this sort of equilibrium is very dysfunctional in today's dynamic environment.

There is a long historic record of ideas being quashed by those in power. Innovative ideas can threaten the status quo. This was the case when Galileo supported Copernican ideas that were contrary to Catholic Church teachings.[41] This phenomenon continues today. Consider North Korea for example. The expression of new ideas from the vast majority of the population is not tolerated. Therefore, the ruling class imposes almost absolute selection against any new idea, and they create an alternative reality with their propaganda machine. In this environment, this nation-state remains stagnant while much of the world advances rapidly.

---

41   Galileo Galilei, *Dialogue Concerning the Two Chief World System: Ptolemaic and Copernican*, ed. Steven Jay Gould, trans. Stillman Drake (New York: Modern Library, 2001).

Similar situations occur in many theocracies, such as the so-called Islamic State or Afghanistan under the Taliban. In these societies, very conservative interpretation of religious teachings makes many new ideas and creative activities taboo. Suppression of new ideas as a tool to maintain the status quo is nothing new. In fact this form of idea stagnation is probably as old as human society. The good news is that over time, idea migration usually overwhelms the ability of totalitarian states and theocracies to suppress ideas. It was the power of ideas that led to the Renaissance, the creation of the United States, and the fall of the Soviet Union. I would further wager that idea migration will eventually overwhelm totalitarian regimes in North Korea and in the Middle East.

While totalitarian nation-states and religion-based censorship are powerful demonstrations of equilibria, similar situations exist within many organizations. Typically, organizations that suffer from this malady tend to be very top-down. Many are small family-owned businesses where virtually every decision is made by the family patriarch. New ideas get nixed simply because of an aversion to change. In some cases, more progressive family members have to wait for the patriarch to retire or die before they can bring new ideas into the fold.

In other cases, pressures against new ideas may come from the rank and file. This is especially the case where employees are very comfortable with the status quo and/or extremely fearful of change. I have observed this scenario most frequently in public agencies and not-for-profits. In these environments, management is often in a weakened state due to organizational culture, political oversight, and boards that constantly meddle and check almost every managerial decision. Employees tend to like the way things are and see no need for change. They also possess enough power to resist new proposals. Sometimes dominant employees even develop back channels to board members to undercut new ideas put forward by management.

In a high-change environment, organizations that approach a state of equilibrium between idea immigration and selection are potentially in a death spiral. Often these organizations need new ideas to survive but create barriers to innovation. Let's consider an example in an iconic American institution.

The US Postal Service is literally as old as the United States. But along the way, it has been repeatedly challenged as communication technologies have improved. At first, the challenges came slowly (the telegraph and telephone). The Postal Service weathered these early storms because it had a substantial cost advantage. But today the Postal Service is confronted with a rapid onslaught of virtually free digital technologies, such as email, texting, social media, online banking and bill payment, and long-distance voice and video communication. Additionally, parcel delivery companies such as UPS and FedEx have greatly impacted the Postal Service's package delivery business. As a result, the total volume of mail sent via the Postal Service declined by 25 percent between 2006 and 2015. Today, personal letters account for only 5 percent of total mail volume, and magazines of all kinds make up only 3.5 percent.[42]

The Postal Service's ability to change has been hampered by local and national politics and by resistance to change from its own rank and file. This has essentially created negative selection against any game-changing ideas, and today the Postal Service is undercapitalized and bleeding red ink. In the meantime, its competition expands and the Digital Revolution marches on, providing new communication technologies every year. The Postal Service finds itself in an idea-driven business sector without the ability to adequately innovate.

Just as in the case of restrictive regimes, the solution to idea equilibria in organizations is to relax the negative selection and accelerate the immigration of viable new ideas. Organizations must be able to innovate in order to survive. Leadership structures must be modified

---

42   Kevin Kosar, "Post Office Continues Sinking as the Band Plays On," *Newsweek*, November 23, 2015, http://www.newsweek.com/post-office-continues-sinking-band-plays-397320.

to facilitate innovation. In Chapter 1, I pointed out that many organizations have completely abandoned hierarchical structures in favor of flatter administrative structures that are more fluid and enable ideas to flow more effectively throughout the organization. In these organizations, innovative concepts are much more likely to win the day. It is no coincidence that most innovative organizations, such as Google, 3M, Adobe, and Cisco, have successfully adopted flatter administrative structures.

Continuous Assessment of the Effectiveness of Ideas

In nature, genes are constantly under pressure. If they do not contribute to the overall fitness of the organism, they become subject to removal by natural selection. In short, nature is always seeking to optimize genetic makeup for specific environmental conditions.

We should similarly never consider ideas to be in a final form. Instead, they should be constantly reviewed to find and correct flaws and to find opportunities for additional improvements. This requires that everyone become engaged in the assessment process.

Dr. W. Edwards Deming played a large role in the post-war development of the automobile industry in Japan and is widely credited with the creation of a culture of constant process improvement. His work largely focused on the continual pursuit of better ideas leading to better processes and better products. Though he focused on industrial systems, his system has broad application in organizations of all types. He summarized his approach with the following fourteen points:

1. Create constancy of purpose toward the improvement of product and service with the aim to become competitive and to stay in business and provide jobs.

2. Adopt the new philosophy. We are in a new economic age. Western management must awaken to the challenge, must learn their responsibilities, and take on leadership for change.

3. Cease dependence on inspection to achieve quality. Eliminate

the need for inspection on a mass basis by building quality into the product in the first place.

4. End the practice of awarding business on the basis of price tag. Instead, minimize total cost. Move toward a single supplier for any one item on a long-term relationship of loyalty and trust.

5. Improve constantly and forever the system of production and service to improve quality and productivity and thus constantly decrease costs.

6. Institute training on the job.

7. Institute leadership. The aim of supervision should be to help people and machines and gadgets to do a better job. Supervision of management is in need of overhaul, as well as supervision of production workers.

8. Drive out fear, so that everyone may work effectively for the company.

9. Break down barriers between departments.

10. Eliminate slogans, exhortations, and targets for the workforce asking for zero defects and new levels of productivity. Such exhortations only create adversarial relationships, as the bulk of the causes of low quality and low productivity belong to the system and thus lie beyond the power of the workforce.

    • Eliminate work standards (quotas) on the factory floor. Substitute leadership.

    • Eliminate management by objective. Eliminate management by numbers, or numerical goals. Substitute leadership.

11. Remove barriers that rob the hourly worker of their right to pride of workmanship. The responsibility of supervisors must be changed from sheer numbers to quality.

12. Remove barriers that rob people in management and in engineering of their right to pride of workmanship. This means, inter alia, the abolishment of the annual or merit

rating and of management by objective.

13. Institute a vigorous program of education and self-improvement.

14. Put everybody in the company to work to accomplish the transformation. The transformation is everybody's job.[43]

Deming's methods apply a holistic approach to identify better ideas leading to process improvement and enhanced quality. He also recognized that idea review is everyone's job and not simply a management function. Everyone should be in constant pursuit of a better way. There is no constancy; everything is under constant review.

In every organization, decisions have to be made regarding which idea will be advanced and which will be tabled or discarded. These decisions must be based upon analysis and critical thought. However, decisions must also be reached in a timely manner. This can only be done when decisions are made closer to the point of origin of the idea. Continuous process assessment creates a unique opportunity for organizations to engage everyone, not only in the development of new ideas but also in the assessment of the viability of both proposed and existing processes. This disperses the decision-making process and shifts it closer to the point of idea origin.

"Making good decisions is a crucial skill at every level."

Peter Drucker

---

43   "Dr. Deming's 14 Points for Management," The W. Edwards Deming Institute, accessed November 9, 2017, https://deming.org/explore/fourteen-points.

Steps You Can Take to Ensure that the Right Ideas Are Supported and Advanced

1. **Base idea selection on critical thought processes, not solely on opinion.**

   - Consider developing a rubric to help managers and employees assess the value of ideas based on logic and evidence instead of gut reaction.

2. **Avoid creating a stagnant environment where most new ideas are summarily killed.**

   - You cannot drive into the future with both eyes fixed on your rearview mirror. Just because your operational strategies were effective in the past does not mean that they remain relevant today and into the future.

   - When you send a signal that you are averse to change, employees become frustrated and creativity is lost.

3. **Develop a process of continuous assessment.**

   - Everyone should have a voice in this process and feel comfortable in making recommendations for change.

   - Every aspect of your organization should be constantly reviewed and be subject to improvement.

CHAPTER 8

How Environmental Quality Affects Rate of Change

G rowing up on a ranch in southwestern New Mexico, I saw the "constancy of change" all around me. When seasonal rains arrived, life was seemingly everywhere. It was almost as if life was hiding somewhere waiting to make its grand entrance. When the dry season arrived, much of the life around me simply disappeared. In the harsh environment of the Chihuahuan Desert, everything was cyclical. Life expanded and contracted in response to these environmental changes. Much later, I learned that these cyclical environmental changes not only caused natural populations to expand and contract, but they also had a massive impact on the rate of genetic change within these populations.

Effect of Environmental Quality on Genetic Change

When times are good during periods of high environmental quality, survival rates are high. The most fit organisms and those of lesser fitness both flourish. In other words, the amount of selection pressure exerted on the species by the environment is minimal. But when food becomes limited, when predators become more prevalent, or when diseases and parasites abound, only the fittest could function in this more challenging environment. In this case, natural selection goes into hyperdrive exerting extreme selection pressure and the rate of genetic change accelerates.

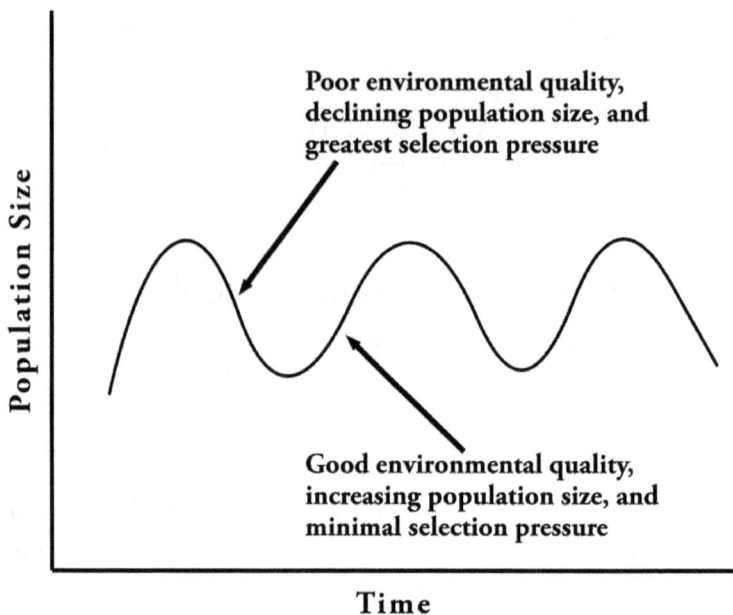

Of course, the ability of a population of organisms to change in response to a declining environmental quality is predicated on the existence of genetic variation. If all members of a population are genetically similar, then a population may be doomed in the face of rapid decline in environmental quality. But if some members of a population have genes that help them survive and sustain under periods of hardship, their genes will be passed to coming generations, and as a result, the population will become more capable of dealing with future environmental challenges. Here is a real-world example.

In my backyard, I have a chronic problem with voles (small burrowing rodents). In some years, the vole population is small, and there is little damage to my yard. In other years, voles seem to be everywhere. Red foxes prey upon the voles, so as long as a sufficient population of foxes is present, vole numbers remain low and manageable. In essence, the foxes exert selection pressure on the voles. More foxes equate to more selection pressure, and voles that lack the ability to avoid the foxes quickly become fox food.

A couple of years ago, our fox population was decimated due to a disease that spread rapidly among the local population. The disease essentially reduced the environmental quality for the foxes and only the foxes with genetic resistance to the disease survived. Conversely, with the rapid decline in foxes, the population of voles expanded rapidly. Their environmental quality suddenly improved. While the foxes were undergoing extreme selection pressure caused by the disease (only a few survived), voles reproduced rapidly. Natural selection on the voles was taking a holiday.

Today, the red fox population is beginning to recover. Their reproductive rates are high. The population now has a high level of resistance to the disease, and there is an abundance of food (voles). In other words, if you are a fox, the environmental quality is very good. The probability of your offspring surviving to adulthood is excellent, and soon we will again have a robust population of foxes. However, if you are a vole, your environmental quality is starting to decline. More foxes equal more selection pressure. In the coming years, only those voles with the ability to evade the foxes will survive.

Impact of Declining Organizational Environmental Quality

In businesses, not-for-profits, and public agencies, environmental changes are also cyclical. Change associated with business cycles, the overall economy, political ideologies, and customer/client preference ebbs and flows. There are times of growth and times of contraction.

As is the case in natural populations, when organizational resources abound, idea selection is minimal. Under these conditions, a lot of ideas may arise and gain traction. Some will be good ideas, and some will be not-so-good ideas. But it is during the downturns that the potential for change is greatest. Under these conditions, only a few ideas will survive and flourish.

As I mentioned earlier, it is diversity in thought and approaches that enables organizational change in response to change in the operational environment. In fact, we are in an era of accelerating change in our operational environments. Organizations must be more dynamic and capable of strategic and tactical change. Diversity of ideas and approaches must exist before an organization can effectively respond to new challenges. During cyclical downturns, this idea variation is even more critical.

Management's role in determining what ideas gain traction in a downturn cannot be understated. During these times, organizations lack the resources to grow, so they begin to contract. Management has to decide which ideas will be kept and which will be lost. Often staffing must be reduced, and when this occurs, ideas are lost as people move on. Massive change is possible when management seizes the opportunity instead of rushing back to some perceived safe harbor in an outdated organizational vision and operational model.

Organizations that emphasize tenure over creativity often fall into this trap. In this case, the longest-serving employees survive the downturn, while those with the least tenure lose their jobs. In our rapidly changing organizational environments, the best ideas may reside with the individuals with less tenure, whereas those with the longest tenure may actually be less creative and more traditional. Therefore, it is imperative that management has the tools necessary to keep those with the ideas and concepts that can drive the organization forward in a challenging environment, while continuing to deliver the goods and services required by clients and customers.

Creating Disruption to Accelerate Organizational Change

Animal and plant breeders have long understood that more progress is possible when the environment is artificially manipulated to create more stress on the organism. However, this environmental manipulation must be done in a very strategic manner. For example, livestock breeders who desire to genetically enhance fertility in their herds accomplish this by ratcheting down the number of days that females are exposed to sires. Under these conditions, only the most fertile females are able to conceive and subsequently produce offspring.

In organizations, disruptions often occur because of external factors, such as budgetary constraints or changes in the economy, supply chains, and customer preference. But the notion of introducing disruptions is also gaining momentum. Organizations that want to accelerate change often seek to accomplish this by creating more pressures to generate and apply new ideas that lead to process improvement.

In a well-managed organization, increased selection pressure can be placed on ideas by engaging in constant and rigorous review. Disruptive managers question the status quo throughout their organization. In this environment, there can be no sacred cows. All units are under constant review and assessment. In other words, all aspects of the organization are expected to be in a constant state of change seeking a better way to function.

Back in chapter 5, I discussed Dr. Deming's approach to constant process improvement.[44] In large measure, this was predicated on creating an environment in which constant disruption thrives. His fourteen-point approach was largely designed to create an environment whereby all aspects of the organization are constantly under review and whereby pressure for change is ever present. For many employees, this sort of an environment seems scary. But when reward systems and training regimes are created to encourage innovation, Deming believed that fear could be "driven out" of the organization even under constant assessment.

Conversely, I have known many managers who pressed employees to change without clearly establishing the rationale and expectations. Furthermore, they did not adequately incentivize constant process improvement through training and reward systems. The result was constant chaos instead of constant process improvement. Employees did not understand why change was necessary and where they fit into the altered organization. They were in a constant state of fear

---

44   W. Edwards Deming Institute, "Dr. Deming's 14 Points."

and often overreacted to every utterance from management.

Entrepreneur and author Faisal Hoque emphasized that managers must exhibit the following five habits to empower employees to thrive under such constant disruption:[45]

1. **Disruptive managers must relentlessly pursue the truth.** They cannot simply operate on their opinions. They must truly pursue the best approaches throughout their organization, constantly testing all assumptions and engaging their teams in their thought processes.

2. **Disruptive managers must guide employees and other stakeholders through chaos.** They need to effectively describe how all changes will align with the organization's direction. This requires constant and effective communication.

3. **Disruptive managers must be decisive.** While every effort must be made to ensure that they reach the right decision, leaders cannot wait until everyone is on board before moving forward.

4. **Disruptive managers break rules and write new ones, but they always explain why.** If employees do not know the new rules of the game, they cannot operate within the new reality.

5. **Disruptive managers thrive on uncertainty.** They must be willing to try new approaches often without fully understanding how something will work out. But this must not be seen as a license to be reckless. Managers must use caution to avoid introducing unnecessary chaos. All new ideas must be subject to constant review and tweaking in order to optimize them. Nothing can be assumed to be perfect on day one.

The bottom line is that change can be accelerated when disruptions are introduced. However, this approach will likely fail, and possibly create major negative ramifications, if managerial wisdom is not

---

45 Faisal Hoque, "5 Habits of Truly Disruptive Leaders," *Fast Company*, accessed November 9, 2015, https://www.fastcompany.com/3052725/5-habits-of-truly-disruptive-leaders.

present. Fear must be driven out of the organization by ensuring that employees fully understand why disruptions are being introduced. They must also understand the potential value to themselves. Management must also make it very clear that training and other support mechanisms will be in place to prepare employees for the new environment of accelerated change. In short, employees must see themselves as change agents with a major role in creating the next iteration of the organization.

"Change is inevitable and the disruption it causes often brings both inconvenience and opportunity."

Robert Scoble

Steps You Can Take to Leverage Disruptions to Accelerate Change

1. **If you create deliberate disruptions, ensure that they are strategic and focus on constant process improvement.**

2. **Ensure that the workforce clearly understands the rationale before introducing disruptions.**

   - Effective communication is critical.

   - Introduction of stressors without a clear understanding of purpose will only create chaos.

   - Communication must be constant and effective.

   - All levels of management must be prepared for the introduction of the disruption.

3. **Avoid promising a specific outcome when disruptions are introduced.**

   - Disruptions will create uncertainty and often take an organization to an unforeseen place.

   - Strive to direct the outcome toward long-term organizational goals.

4. **Make every effort to drive out fear of change.**

   - Employees must understand why change is needed.

   - Successes should be celebrated.

   - Reward systems must be clearly defined. Employees must understand the value they derive from pursuing process improvement.

   - Training must be readily available to help employees assess process effectiveness, recommend changes, and adjust the nature of their work as changes are implemented.

5. **Carefully assess each change resulting from the introduction of a disruptive force to ensure that it is beneficial to the organization.**

   • Do not expect every new concept to be perfect on day one. Tweaking should always be expected as new approaches are implemented.

   • Follow the initiation of any change with assessment. This will likely lead to additional change and additional assessments— or in other words, *constant process improvement*.

6. **Use Deming's fourteen-point approach as a guide to how to introduce and manage disruptions (see chapter 7).**

CHAPTER 9

Eliminating Idea Death and Optimizing Employee Turnover Rate

In most organizations, employees will have various responses to change. Some will readily embrace change and seek constant innovation; some will fear change, thrive on constancy, and generally prefer to simply follow orders. As I discussed in earlier chapters, constant process improvement is predicated on the notion that everyone is an agent of change. So how does it affect an organization when you have a large portion of employees who are not engaged in the creation and application of new ideas? Once again, we can learn from nature.

In nature, the rate of evolutionary change in a population is greatly impacted by two interconnected elements. The first is the portion of the population that is "genetically dead," and the second is the time that is required for one generation to be replaced by the next.

Genetic Death: Failure to Contribute Genes to the Next Generation

In nature, organisms which are not able to reproduce are said to be "genetically dead." This doesn't mean that they are physically dead. In fact, genetically dead organisms are very much alive. They consume resources, but they are unable to contribute genes to the next generation.

Generally, genetic death is caused by the inability to compete for mates, by sterility, or in some cases, by choice. In some species, the number of individuals in a state of genetic death is minimal. For example, some insects die shortly after mating. In other species, such as humans, the majority of the population may be genetically dead.

According to the National Center for Health Statistics,[46] the average age of mothers and fathers at the birth of a child is 26.3 and 27.4, respectively. And the vast majority of births occur when parents are less than 35 years of age. However, fully 54 percent of the population of the US is over 35 years of age. The vast majority of these individuals are genetically dead given that they will not produce additional offspring.

When a large percentage of a population is in a state of genetic death, this can negatively impact the rate of genetic change (evolution). In nature, genetically dead organisms compete for resources, leaving fewer resources for those capable of reproduction. Organisms that are nutritionally stressed may not be able to reproduce or may produce smaller numbers of progeny. In some cases, genetically dead individuals may even interfere with the mating processes of others. Consider the sterile bull elk that gathers a harem and fights off fertile competitors during the breeding season.

Idea Death: Failure to Support the Organization's Future

When individuals in the workplace no longer generate and advance new ideas, their contribution to the organization's future is minimized. In essence, they are in a state of "idea death." In some organizations, idea death begins on day one of employment when there is no

---

46   T. J. Mathews and B. E. Hamilton, *Mean Age of Mothers Is on the Rise: United States, 2000–2014* (Hyattsville, MD: National Center for Health Statistics, 2016), https://www.cdc.gov/nchs/products/databriefs/db232. htm.

expectation of innovation associated with the position. In other cases, formerly innovative employees lose the ability to innovate as their careers advance and drift into a state of idea death over time.

In a high-change environment, every employee must contribute to the organization's idea pool. We no longer have the luxury of having people simply show up and do the work. In the words of Deming, you must "put everybody in the company to work to accomplish the transformation. The transformation is everybody's job."[47] The transformation that Deming described is the constant process of improvement leading to the production of the highest-quality products and services. This requires everyone's ideas.

During my years in academia, I observed a conscious effort to reduce the rate of idea death among faculty. Early on I noticed that the productivity of a significant proportion of fully promoted and tenured faculty began to noticeably "taper off" toward the end of their careers. They arrived to work later and left earlier; and more importantly, their contribution of new ideas declined dramatically. This decline was largely accepted and in a sense seen as an earned benefit.

Post-tenure review processes have now been initiated at many universities. These processes are designed to make it more difficult for individuals to check out long before retirement. Some institutions have reduced the number of faculty eligible for tenure. Some have also leveraged early retirement incentives to help move senior faculty out and make room for new junior faculty who bring with them the latest skills and ideas. The net effect in academia has been a marked decline in idea death coupled with an increased rate of idea migration.

In all organizations, collective brainpower is a resource that should never be allowed to decline. Therefore, idea death must be limited. Employees must have access to high-quality training and education to avoid declines in knowledge, skills, problem-solving abilities, and creativity. Management should see training and education as an

47   W. Edwards Deming Institute, "Dr. Deming's 14 Points."

investment in the capacity of the organization and not as a cost to the organization.

Organizational structures should also facilitate interaction among employees and cultivate exchange of ideas. Think back to the case of the Post-it Note. It was a seminar that connected Silver's adhesive microsphere concept with someone from another part of the 3M organization who had a need. Whether through formal seminars, assignment to diverse teams, or any other activities that bring employees together to share ideas and needs, mixing is a good thing.

Idea inbreeding and idea death share an antidote—idea churn. When you couple migration of new ideas into an organization with exchange of ideas within the organization, you have a powerful tool for minimizing both idea inbreeding and idea death.

Simply stated, idea death can be reduced by keeping everyone engaged and equipped to contribute ideas to the organization. But when all else fails, those without viable ideas may need to move on to make room for new personnel who are able to help the organization enhance the quality of its products and service.

Optimizing Rate of Personnel Turnover

Under some conditions, the rate of evolutionary change or directed change in domesticated species can be greatly impacted by the rate of generation turnover. The rate of generation turnover varies greatly from species to species. Human generations are replaced in twenty to twenty-five years. At the other end of the spectrum, bacteria can replace a generation in a matter of minutes.

The impact of generation turnover on genetic change is not universal. There are some conditions in which accelerating generation turnover greatly impacts rate of change, while there are other conditions where a change in generation turnover has essentially no effect.

Animal species that reproduce sexually provide perhaps the best platform to understand when rapid turnover accelerates change and when it has only a negligible effect. To demonstrate this, let's consider two herds of beef cattle.

In the first herd, there is little selection pressure exerted by the owner of the herd. The owner purchases breeding bulls from another herd, but the genetic merit of these bulls is very similar to that of his overall herd. Therefore, the average genetic merit of calves is very similar to that of both of their parents.

In the second herd, the owner carefully selects the very best breeding bulls from other herds. He also utilizes artificial insemination which allows him to access the very best genetics available. In other words, high-quality genes are regularly migrating into the herd because of intensive selection of breeding bulls and semen. As a result, the average genetic merit of these immigrant sires far exceeds the average genetic merit of the females to which they are mated. And the genetic merit of the calves substantially exceeds that of their mothers.

If we accelerate the rate of generation turnover in the first herd, we will simply be replacing one generation with another of similar genetic merit. Therefore, accelerated turnover has little effect. Conversely, when females in the second herd are turned over more rapidly, they are replaced by superior offspring. As a result, the rate of genetic change accelerates.

On the surface, it seems that the decision to accelerate turnover is an easy one. However, cattle breeders will tell you that it is not so simple. It takes approximately two years before a replacement female has its first calf. It also takes about five years for a replacement female to achieve maximum production potential. Since cattle producers are paid based on the weight of the calves they produce, this loss of productivity affects their sales volume and their bottom line. The development of a replacement animal also requires more nutritional and managerial inputs. This equates to increased costs. All of this needs to be weighed against the value of an enhanced rate of genetic change.

In organizations, turnover is accomplished when employees are replaced by new hires. According to the Bureau of Labor Statistics, the median tenure for all employees in the US was 4.2 years in 2016. Among public employees, federal and local government employees have the longest tenures (8.9 and 8.8 years, respectively), while state employees tend to have much lower tenures. Private sector tenure is greatest in manufacturing (5.3 years) and lowest in leisure and hospitality occupations (2.2 years).[48]

Remember that employees are vessels of ideas, knowledge, and skills. Therefore, the potential for gain resulting from accelerated turnover is largely determined by the rate at which new ideas, knowledge, and skills migrate into the organization with new employees. If new hires bring superior skills, knowledge, and ideas, then there is considerable value in accelerating turnover. Conversely, if new hires are largely trained on the job and require an extended period of time to reach the average capability of existing employees, accelerating turnover will have little impact and may actually have a detrimental effect. Additionally, when long-tenured employees leave, organizational knowledge and wisdom may also be lost.

Obviously, there is a relationship between turnover rate and idea death. In an organization with a high incidence of idea death, higher turnover can have a very positive impact on innovation. Of course, this is contingent upon new hires being more innovative than those who are idea dead. It is also important to keep in mind that turnover in organizations has some of the same costs as those incurred in my cattle breeding example. The cost needs to be balanced against the value of more rapid change in skills, ideas, and knowledge.

Early on, new employees are usually not as productive as more experienced personnel, so there may be a short-term loss in productivity associated with turnover. Additionally, there are significant costs associated with developing the replacement. These

---

48   Bureau of Labor Statistics, "Employee Tenure in 2016," news release no. USDL-16-1867, September 22, 2016, https://www.bls.gov/news.release/pdf/tenure.pdf.

include recruitment, orientation, and training. Additionally, accelerating turnover rate can unnecessarily instill a sense of insecurity among employees. This is especially the case when individuals do not know where they stand in the minds of management. Awareness of these costs may temper the desire for maximum turnover, even when it appears warranted based on the potential for change.

Generally, organizations do not maintain high turnover rates indefinitely. Accelerating turnover is generally a corrective measure to better align staffing with the present and future needs of the organization. An organization with continued rapid turnover quite likely has other problems, such as an inability to attract and adequately train new employees. An organization with sustained high turnover rates also likely has issues with morale, quality assurance, and customer satisfaction. Additionally, when management is not capable of adequately assessing the difference between highly skilled and innovative employees from those in a state of idea death, accelerated turnover will have no net effect.

There are six key questions that determine the optimal rate of turnover. Responses to these questions can help determine if the turnover rate should be slowed or accelerated.

1. Are your short-tenured employees more creative and productive than your long-tenured employees?

◄— Slower Turnover		Quicker Turnover —►	
Long-tenured employees are most creative and productive.	Long-tenured employees are somewhat more creative and productive.	Short-tenured employees are slightly more creative and productive than longer-tenured employees.	Short-tenured employees are more productive and creative than longer-tenured employees.

2. How difficult and expensive is it to recruit highly skilled, knowledgeable, and innovative employees?

← Slower Turnover		Quicker Turnover →	
Very Difficult—Candidates with necessary attributes are not available, and expensive on-the-job training is necessary.	Somewhat Difficult—A limited pool of candidates is available. Much on-the-job training is necessary.	Relatively Easy—A large pool of candidates is available, and limited on-the-job training is necessary.	Very Easy—A large pool of highly qualified candidates is available, and they can contribute immediately.

3. How do the skills, knowledge, and creativity of your current employees compare to your competitors?

← Slower Turnover		Quicker Turnover →	
Current employees are far superior to those in competing organizations.	Current employees are somewhat superior to those in competing organizations.	Current employees are somewhat inferior to those in competing organizations.	Current employees are generally inferior to those in competing organizations.

4. Do new employees make mistakes and compromise product/service quality?

← Slower Turnover		Quicker Turnover →	
New employees make more frequent mistakes and require extensive supervision.	New employees make occasional mistakes and require a moderate degree of supervision.	New employees make no more mistakes than long-tenured employees and require only modest supervision.	New employees make very few mistakes and tend to outperform long-tenured employees.

5. How difficult is it to fire employees lacking skill, knowledge, and creativity?

←— Slower Turnover		Quicker Turnover —→	
Very Difficult—A cumbersome process must be followed.	Somewhat Difficult—Substantial documentation is needed.	Relatively Easy—Some process is still required.	Very Easy—All employees are subject to immediate dismissal.

6. How difficult and expensive is it to accelerate retirement?

←— Slower Turnover		Quicker Turnover —→	
Very Difficult—Organizational rules limit payment of incentives.	Somewhat Difficult—Incentive payments are limited to modest amounts.	Relatively Easy—Budgetary resources are, however, somewhat limited.	Easy—Resources are available for substantial incentives.

There are additional factors that affect turnover rate which are specific to each organization. For example, higher turnover rates occur in organizations with inferior compensation packages (salaries and benefits) and poor work environments. These are issues that must be independently resolved in order to effectively compete for new talent and to retain your best existing talent.

Nevertheless, every organization should strive to optimize turnover for their specific conditions. This will improve productivity and competitiveness.

"I like to stay busy, I like to stay focused, and I like to stay creative.

Without being creative, I'd be dead."

Jeremy Renner

Steps You Can Take to Eliminate Idea Death and to Optimize Turnover Rate

Eliminate Idea Death

1. **Encourage engagement in creative activities.**

   - Consistently and continually stress the importance of everyone's ideas.

   - Do not allow a culture to develop wherein employees find it advantageous to keep their heads down and just do their jobs instead of seeking process improvements.

2. **Do not allow ideas of employees to be stifled by peers.**

   - No not allow dominant workers who fear change to suppress ideas of others.

   - Help younger and more introverted employees find their voice and advance their ideas.

   - Feature more introverted employees in presentations and in other in-house media.

   - Carefully create teams and working groups to minimize the dominance effect.

3. **Provide opportunities for employees to acquire the knowledge and skills that they need to fully develop and deploy their ideas.**

   - Knowledge is in large measure a prerequisite for innovation. If employees do not fully understand a problem or opportunity, they will likely not be able to develop a viable innovation.

4. **Do not allow longer-tenured employees to linger without an expectation of creativity.**

   - Honor past contributions, but do not create a sense that the organization owes them the right to taper off in their later years.

5. **Make creativity a core value of the organization, and equip every employee to contribute to the innovative processes.**

   • Do not simply acknowledge employees. Empower them by changing the culture and encouraging everyone to put forward innovative ideas and process improvements.

   • Create channels of communication to ensure that ideas and recommendations from every employee are presented to appropriate decision makers.[49]

6. **Evaluate managers based upon the innovation and creativity expressed in their respective units.**

7. **Evaluate employees not only on the quality of their work but also on their efforts to improve the effectiveness of the organization.**

Optimizing Turnover Rate

1. **Accelerate turnover when an organization is in need of rapid change in order to effectively respond to challenges and opportunities and when ideas must change as rapidly as possible.**

   • Once new concepts have been identified that will propel the organization forward, those who cannot support these concepts because they are unable to or unwilling to acquire necessary skills or knowledge may need to leave the organization.

2. **Do not accelerate turnover when management lacks a clear vision for the organization's future. In this case, accelerated turnover may be detrimental to positive change.**

   • Leadership should control the rudder and have a clear notion as to the long-term goals and objectives of the organization.

---

49 John Hunter, "Deming and Lean: Disparities and Similarities," *The W. Edwards Deming Institute Blog*, The W. Edwards Deming Institute, July 8, 2013, https://blog.deming.org/2013/07/deming-and-lean-the-disparities-and-similaritie

- Yogi Berra is often quoted as saying, "You've got to be very careful if you don't know where you are going, because you might not get there."[50] If you initiate accelerated turnover without a clear notion of the direction, you will likely end up even worse off than before. New people will enter the organization without a clear notion of direction, and their innovation will not be focused on the greater mission of the organization.

3. **Accelerate turnover when applicant pools are very strong and when new hires bring significant new skills, knowledge, and creativity into the organization.**

   - Weigh short-term costs associated with recruitment and lower initial productivity of new hires against long-term gains to the organization.

4. **Do not accelerate turnover when the number and quality (in terms of skills, knowledge, and creativity) of applicants are lacking as compared to that of existing employees.**

   - Give people with flawed or underdeveloped ideas a chance to improve by providing opportunities for professional development and positive, factual feedback, and encourage everyone to work in team settings. It is possible to turnover ideas without necessarily turning over employees.

5. **If turnover is not a management decision but is instead caused by loss of high-quality employees to other organizations, managers must discover the reasons and find remedies. Otherwise, you will become a training ground for your competitors.**

   - Constantly evaluate how your salary and benefits' structures compare to your competitors' frameworks.

   - Conduct effective exit interviews with departing employees to ascertain why they are leaving.

---

50   Nate Scott, "The 50 Greatest Yogi Berra Quotes," *USA Today*, September 23, 2015, http://ftw.usatoday.com/2015/09/the-50-greatest-yogi-berra-quotes.

- Seek to maintain diversity in your organization. If those departing are more diverse than those remaining, you are on a dangerous trajectory. Find out why these individuals were not comfortable within your organization.

CONCLUSION

The great philosopher Yogi Berra once said that "the future ain't what it used to be."[51] As with many "Yogi-isms," this statement is loaded with irony, relevance, and a bit of humor. For thousands of years of human history, change came very slowly—so slowly that it was often unnoticed during the course of our distant ancestors' lifetimes. Therefore, the future was pretty much like the present and the past. So I guess that the future was pretty much what it used to be. But in modern times, Yogi's observation rings true. Today, the present is very different from even the very recent past. And in all likelihood, the future will be massively different from the present. So the future definitely ain't what it used to be.

We have to recognize that the attributes of the future are largely unknown. Much like a meteorologist, we can make projections based on available information. But as is the case with weather forecasts, the precision of these predictions rapidly diminishes as we look further and further ahead. The only certainty is that there will be changes.

Some see the future through a very dark and ominous lens, envisioning

---

51   Scott, "Yogi Berra Quotes."

what's to come as a big hairy demon hiding in the shadows. In Charles Dickens's A Christmas Carol, there were three ghosts representing the phases of Scrooge's life—past, present, and future. But it is the ghost representing the future that is the scariest of the three. He emerges as a Grim Reaper-like character reflecting a very negative view of the future. But interestingly, this apparition also relates hope to Scrooge. A positive outcome is possible, but only if he is able to change.[52] The future holds many big hairy demon-like challenges, but it also holds many opportunities for those who confront the status quo. To avoid the big hairy demon version of the future, we must embrace constant change and adjust to these new realities.

As I discussed in this book, nature provides the basis by which environmental change can be quickly sensed and by which positive response can occur. But this response requires genetic diversity. If all organisms in a population are genetically similar, the population will likely become extinct in the face of rapid environmental change. Healthy living populations are diverse and also have permeable borders that allow migrants to enter the population. These immigrants inject new genetic variation and make the population more resilient in the face of new environmental challenges.

Living populations have built-in sensors to detect even minor changes in the environment. As the environment changes, individuals with the right genes produce more offspring. Their descendants are also more likely to become the parents of subsequent generations. In essence, the population senses the change and expands the number of individuals who are best equipped to flourish in the new environment. Additionally, the rate of genetic change accelerates as the intensity of the environmental pressure increases. Individuals who are not suited for the radically new environment either die off or reproduce at lower rates than those with the right genes. Under these conditions, generations turn over more rapidly, further

---

52   Charles Dickens, *A Christmas Carol* (London, 1843).

accelerating the rate of genetic change. When more rapid genetic change is needed, nature delivers.

In your organization, the future need not be a big hairy demon. Instead, it can be a very positive place and deliver many new opportunities. But much like Scrooge, you will have to change. What works today will soon be archaic. And as change accelerates, your organization will have to also change constantly and quickly. It will be ideas that drive these changes.

Your employees are the vessels holding these ideas. In most organizations, some of these vessels are overflowing while others may be nearly empty. The most successful organizations in a high-change environment are those with the best and most applicable ideas. But diversity of the ideas held in these vessels is critical; if all of the vessels hold identical ideas, your organization will fail as the environment changes. You simply cannot expect to change if diversity of thought (the fuel for change) is lacking. Your employees need to possess a variety of ideas and approaches. Don't expect this variation to occur if hiring practices and employee development processes emphasize uniformity and a predestined organizational culture.

Idea diversity is created when new ideas readily flow into the organization from the outside, adding to the vessels or replacing existing ideas that are flawed or outdated. Idea migration obliterates the negative effects caused by isolation. In essence, migration reconnects the isolated entity to the broader world—enhancing interconnectivity and idea exchange. Migratory processes are maximized when recruitment processes support hiring a diverse workforce, when a culture that honors diversity is cultivated and maintained, and when employees are given opportunities to pursue new ideas and training outside of the organization.

Rapid and positive change will only occur when leadership is complementary and visionary. When new ideas are quickly quashed by leadership, innovation will die. Employees must not be just given permission to be creative; they must be allowed to readily seek new ideas. Furthermore, leadership should support and nurture the emerging ideas. These processes are augmented when flatter leadership models are employed. Structures that shift power away from the executive suite and closer to the rank and file facilitate more rapid emergence, expression, and support of new ideas.

Management controls the purse strings and therefore has significant say in what ideas are advanced and which are tabled or discarded. This is an awesome responsibility in times of rapid and constant change. Managers must be unbiased and listen to ideas emerging from across the organization. Ideas should not only come from the influential and the most persuasive. Decision processes should ensure that these decisions are based on critical thought and not gut reaction.

Change becomes more fluid when a culture of constant process improvement permeates the organization.[53] When all processes are exposed to constant review with an eye toward improvement, employees will begin to bring forward ideas as to how their jobs could be done more effectively. Organizational culture must not only empower them to seek new solutions, but it must also create channels for them to quickly bring their recommendations to decision makers.

Disruptions often accelerate change. These can be introduced into an organization either deliberately by management or by external forces. When management deliberately introduces a disruption, the rationale must be clearly communicated, and employees must be supported as they strive to respond to the disruption. Generally, these disruptions require employees to increase their focus on processes within the organization.

Constant process improvement requires the engagement of *all*

---

53   Matt Wrye, "Survival Is Not Mandatory," *Beyond Lean* (blog), September 2, 2013, https://beyondlean.wordpress.com/2013/09/02/survival-is-not-mandatory/; Lean Manufacturing Junction, "Key Lean Manufacturing Principles," accessed November 9, 2017, http://www.lean-manufacturing-junction.com/lean-manufacturing-principles.html; W. Edwards Deming Institute, "Dr. Deming's 14 Points."

employees to examine processes and seek ways to enhance efficiency, process flow, and product/service quality. Training must be available to employees to enable them to perform this task. Those who cannot or will not participate in process improvement may need to leave the organization. In other words, idea death must be minimized if not completely eliminated. But accelerating turnover will only be effective when it is possible to replace those in a persistent state of idea death with new employees who can quickly contribute to the organization's idea pool and actively engage in process improvement.

Humans are odd creatures. We seek a safe harbor where we can enjoy constancy. But this constancy holds us back and limits our progress. We simultaneously crave new things, new knowledge, new experiences, and better services. The words of Ralph Waldo Emerson address this dichotomy:

> *A foolish consistency is the hobgoblin of little minds, adored by little statesmen and philosophers and divines. With consistency a great soul has simply nothing to do. He may as well concern himself with his shadow on the wall. Speak what you think now in hard words, and tomorrow speak what tomorrow thinks in hard words again, though it contradict everything you said today.—"Ah, so you shall be sure to be misunderstood."—Is it so bad, then, to be misunderstood? Pythagoras was misunderstood, and Socrates, and Jesus, and Luther, and Copernicus, and Galileo, and Newton, and every pure and wise spirit that ever took flesh. To be great is to be misunderstood.*[54]

It is the pursuit of the new and the better that drives us forward. New ideas are often misunderstood, but we cannot dismiss alternative approaches out of hand. Society craves innovations that solve our problems, cure our ailments, and improve the quality of our lives. These desires send feedback to our organizations demanding that we constantly improve the products and services that we provide. If your organization doesn't satisfy this desire, your competitors will.

---

54   Ralph Waldo Emerson, *Self-Reliance and Other Essays* (New York, 1844).

"Nothing new ever happened before."

Benjamin Ferencz

BIBLIOGRAPHY

3M. "History Timeline: Post-it Notes." Accessed November 9, 2017. http://www.post-it.com/3M/en_US/post-it/contact-us/about-us/.

Alzforum. "PSEN1 E280A (Paisa)." Accessed November 9, 2016. http://www.alzforum.org/mutation/psen1-e280a-paisa.

Anthony, Scott. "Stop Inbreeding Innovation." *Harvard Business Review*, March 30, 2012.

Blackerby, Phillip. "History of Strategic Planning." Blackerby Associates. Accessed November 9, 2017. http://www.blackerbyassoc.com/history.html.

Bureau of Labor Statistics. "Employee Tenure in 2016." News release no. USDL-16-1867. September 22, 2016. https://www.bls.gov/news.release/pdf/tenure.pdf.

Cystic Fibrosis Foundation. "About Cystic Fibrosis." Accessed November 9, 2017. https://www.cff.org/What-is-CF/About-Cystic-Fibrosis/.

Darwin, Charles. *On the Origin of Species by Means of Natural Selection*. New York, 1859.

Dickens, Charles. *A Christmas Carol*. London, 1843.

Emerson, Ralph Waldo. *Self-Reliance and Other Essays*. New York, 1844.

Francione, Peter A. *The Delphi Report—Critical Thinking: A Statement of Expert Consensus for Purposes of Educational Assessment and Instruction*. Insight Assessment. November 1989. https://www.researchgate.net/profile/Peter_Facione/publication/242279575_Critical_Thinking_A_Statement_of_Expert_Consensus_for_Purposes_of_Educational_Assessment_and_Instruction/links/5849b94508ae82313e7108de/Critical-Thinking-A-Statement-of-Expert-Consensus-for-Purposes-of-Educational-Assessment-and-Instruction.pdf.

Friedman, Thomas L. *Thank You for Being Late: An Optimist's Guide to Thriving in the Age of Accelerations*. New York: Farrar, Straus and Giroux, 2016.

Galilei, Galileo. *Dialogue Concerning the Two Chief World System: Ptolemaic and Copernican*. Edited by Steven Jay Gould. Translated by Stillman Drake. New York: Modern Library, 2001.

Gilovich, Thomas. *How We Know What Isn't So*. New York: Simon and Schuster, 1991.

Goodwin, Tom. "The Battle Is for the Customer Interface." *Tech Crunch*, March 3, 2015. https://techcrunch.com/2015/03/03/in-the-age-of-disintermediation-the-battle-is-all-for-the-customer-interface/.

Gustin, Sam. "In Kodak Bankruptcy, Another Casualty of the Digital Revolution." *Time Magazine*, January 20, 2012.

Harari, Yuval. *Sapiens: A Brief History of Humankind*. New York: Harper Collins, 2015.

Hardy, G. H. "Mendelian Proportions in a Mixed Population." *Science* 28 (1908): 49–50.

Hoque, Faisal. "5 Habits of Truly Disruptive Leaders." *Fast Company*, November 9, 2015. https://www.fastcompany.com/3052725/5-habits-of-truly-disruptive-leaders.

Hunt, Vivian, Dennis Layton, and Sara Prince. "Why Diversity

Matters." McKinsey and Company. January 2015. http://www.
mckinsey.com/business-functions/organization/our-insights/
why-diversity-matters.

Hunter, John. "Deming and Lean: Disparities and Similarities." *The W. Edwards Deming Institute Blog.* The W. Edwards Deming Institute. July 8, 2013. https://blog.deming.org/2013/07/deming-and-lean-the-disparities-and-similarities/.

IBM. "The Birth of the IBM PC." Accessed November 9, 2017. https://www- 03.ibm.com/ibm/history/exhibits/pc25/pc25_birth.html.

Indiana University. "Some Phenotypes and Their Explanations." Accessed November 9, 2017. http://www.indiana.edu/~oso/lessons/Genetics/Phenotypes.html.

Insight Assessment. "The Holistic Critical Thinking Scoring Rubric—HCTSR." Accessed November 9, 2017. file:///C:/Users/John/Downloads/HCTSR+2014+Insight+Assessment%20(5).pdf.

Isaacson, Walter. *Steve Jobs.* New York: Simon and Schuster, 2011.

Kettlewell, H. B. D. "Darwin's Missing Evidence." *Scientific American* 200 (1959): 48–53.

—. "Further Selection Experiments on Industrial Melanism in the Lepidoptera." *Heredity* 10 (1956): 287–301.

Kosar, Kevin. "Post Office Continues Sinking as the Band Plays On." *Newsweek*, November 23, 2015. http://www.newsweek.com/post-office-continues-sinking-band-plays-397320.

Lean Manufacturing Junction. "Key Lean Manufacturing Principles." Accessed November 9, 2017. http://www.lean-manufacturing-junction.com/lean-manufacturing-principles.html.

Lenzner, Robert. "40% of the Largest US Companies Founded by Immigrants or Their Children." *Forbes Magazine*, April 25, 2013.

Maclean, Norman. *A River Runs through It*. Chicago: University of Chicago Press, 1976.

Mathews, T. J., and B. E. Hamilton. *Mean Age of Mothers Is on the Rise: United States, 2000–2014*. NCHS Data Brief No. 232. Hyattsville, MD: National Center for Health Statistics, 2016. https://www.cdc.gov/nchs/products/databriefs/db232.htm.

Moore, Amy. "Complete Guide to Apple Park." Macworld. September 25, 2017. http://www.macworld.co.uk/feature/apple/52-facts-about-apples-spaceship-campus-february-drone-video-3489704/.

Moore, Gordon. "Cramming More Components onto Integrated Circuits." *Electronics Magazine* 38, no. 9 (April 19, 1965).

Moore, James F. *The Death of Competition: Leadership and Strategy in the Age of Business Ecosystems*. New York: Harper Collins, 1996.

Morgan, Jacob. *The Future of Work: Attract New Talent, Build Better Leaders, and Create a Competitive Organization*. Hoboken, NJ: John Wiley and Sons, 2014.

Neilson, Gary L., Bruce A. Pasternack, and Decio Mendes. "The Four Bases of Organizational DNA." *Strategy + Business* 33 (Winter 2003). http://www.strategy-business.com/article/03406?gko=4f38.

Nienaber Clarke, Jeanee, and Daniel McCool. *Staking Out the Terrain: Power Differentials among Natural Resource Management Agencies*. Albany, NY: State University of New York Press, 1985.

PBS. "Leonardo, the Man Who Saved Science." *Secrets of the Dead*. Aired April 5, 2017. http://www.pbs.org/wnet/secrets/leonardo-man-saved-science-preview/3462/.

—. "The Television Program Transcripts: Part II." *Triumph of the Nerds*. Interview by Robert X. Cringely. Aired June 1996. http://pbs.org/nerds/part2.html.

Puiu, Tibi. "Your Smartphone Is Millions of Times More Powerful than All of NASA's Combined Computing in 1969." *ZME Science*, September 10, 2017. http://www.zmescience.com/research/technology/smartphone-power-compared-to-apollo-432/.

Reuters. "Genetically Modified Animals." July 25, 2013. http://www.reuters.com/news/picture/genetically-modified-animals?articleId=USRTXTZ7A.

Scott, Nate. "The 50 Greatest Yogi Berra Quotes." *USA Today*, September 23, 2015. http://ftw.usatoday.com/2015/09/the-50-greatest-yogi-berra-quotes.

Shakespeare, William. *Macbeth*. New York: Dover, 1993.

Shoffner, Wilson A. *The Military Decision-Making Process: Time for Change*. Monograph for School of Advanced Military Studies, US Army Command and General Staff College, Fort Leavenworth, KS, First Term AY 99-00. file:///C:/Users/Owner/Downloads/ADA381816.pdf.

US Department of Agriculture. Plant and Animal Genetic Resources Preservation: Fort Collins, CO. Accessed November 9, 2017. https://www.ars.usda.gov/plains-area/fort-collins-co/center-for-agricultural-resources-research/plant-and-animal-genetic-resources-preservation/.

The W. Edwards Deming Institute. "Dr. Deming's 14 Points for Management." Accessed November 9, 2017. https://deming.org/explore/fourteen-points.

Weinberg, W. "Über den Nachweis der Vererbung beim Menschen." *Jahreshefte des Vereins Varterländische Naturkunde in Württemberg* 64 (1908): 369–382.

Williams, Thomas N., and Stephen K. Obaro. "Sickle Cell Disease and Malaria Morbidity: A Tale of Two Tails." *Trends in Parasitology* 27, no. 7 (2011): 315.

Wrye, Matt. "Survival Is Not Mandatory." *Beyond Lean* (blog). September 2, 2013. https://beyondlean.wordpress.com/2013/09/02/survival-is-not-mandatory/.

ABOUT THE AUTHOR

John Winder grew up on a cattle ranch in southwestern New Mexico. His experiences during these formative years led to a strong interest in biology and agricultural sciences. He pursued these interests and received his bachelor's and master's degrees at New Mexico State University focusing on animal sciences and genetics.

After completing his master's degree, John advised and assisted agricultural enterprises in Oklahoma and owned and managed his own businesses in New Mexico and Colorado. This provided him with important exposure to the challenges of managing labor, finances, and risk. These experiences also instilled in him a keen awareness of the need for constant innovation and proactive change.

John's experiences also aroused a strong interest in expanding his knowledge base. This led him to return to college and pursue a doctorate in animal breeding and genetics at Colorado State University. After which he held faculty appointments, consultancies, and senior leadership roles at major public land-grant universities, a large nonprofit foundation, and a privately funded public service organization. His leadership responsibilities in these organizations included personnel management and professional development, oversight of multimillion-dollar budgets, development of communications strategies and technologies, accountability for program outcomes, and creation and implementation of long-term plans.

Throughout his career, John was appointed to statewide, multistate, and national boards, commissions, and advisory councils. These provided input to and governance for large natural resources, education, and public service organizations. In this capacity, he was also responsible for evaluating numerous funding proposals, assessing outcomes of programs conducted by the organizations, and providing feedback to organizational leadership.

John and his wife, Patty, live in McCall, Idaho.

www.ingramcontent.com/pod-product-compliance
Lightning Source LLC
Chambersburg PA
CBHW070934210326
41520CB00021B/6933